Home

How I learnt not to run away

Diana Crampton

Home

Published by The Conrad Press in the United Kingdom 2020

Tel: +44(0)1227 472 874
www.theconradpress.com
info@theconradpress.com

ISBN 978-1-913567-30-9

Typesetting and Cover Design by:
Charlotte Mouncey, www.bookstyle.co.uk

The Conrad Press logo was designed by Maria Priestley.

Printed and bound in Great Britain by Clays Ltd, Elcograf S.p.A.

Home

How I learnt not to run away

Diana Crampton

To my sons and their father

Introduction

'Mme Salminen took a particular interest in people who exhibited signs of extreme emotion: it was her belief that violent passions, when efficiently channelled, can create the conditions for what she called 'psychic breakthroughs'.

Amitav Ghosh, *The Calcutta Chromosome*, Picador 1995

Today, I am convinced that the notion of home is a total luxury. They say that the number of people on the move from the Middle East is of biblical proportions; they are fleeing war, but aiming to settle somewhere peaceful and safe. People are migrating around Africa like never before. Day after day, boatloads of people are found adrift in the Mediterranean.

In 2014, Jonathan Dean reports, 50 million people were on the move, more than at any other time since World War II. Five years later and the numbers have swelled to 70 million (UNHCR statistics). On the shores of the Channel a refugee camp called The Jungle 'houses', in plastic shelters, thousands wishing to reach the UK to make a home. Periodically these are torn down and refugees moved on. Dinghies are frequently found trying to cross the Channel, one of the busiest ship thoroughfares in the world. Would the people feel as if they are home when they get to UK?

I have been walking around thinking of this notion of home for several days now. Mainly I had written a memoir twenty years ago and wanted to get it published. The core of the memoir was my instability and mental health, loosely wrapped around notions of emigration, travel, tourism, wandering which I had studied for my Ph.D.

Ultimately the memoir was too personal, perhaps written only for myself and difficult to put in terms that might be of use. My latter intention had been to show that one may have a serious mental illness and still survive. I survived what the health services have called suicide attempts, three of them, although only one was an actual conscious bid to imbibe enough pills to kill me. My father saved me. One of two times I have seen him cry.

The fact remains that a major slant in the older memoir was travel. Here, today, I propose to express what home has meant to me through my life, investigating whether having a sense of home allays mental instability and hence giving us cause to stop and ponder how the world's homeless will progress. How do people create a sense of home? Do they need it?

Why should you read me? I am no celebrity, although I might be known by a small number of readers of the magazine I contribute to. My aim: to try and offer hope for those in the hopeless depths of depression and psychosis, or people who are near them, relatives, friends. My themes are those of relating the instability to either fight or flight and how these are intertwined in my personal history, hoping that readers will find resonances with their own travels or travails.

On my worst days, my poor dear mother, trying hard to buoy me up, would say 'one door closes, another door opens'. It's a good philosophy to live by.

Chapter One

Suburbs

I recall a snippet that the British on average move house once every seven years. On the other hand, the Triestini that I know, from the other half of my heritage, my Italian mother's side, have all been in their abodes for a lifetime, several lifetimes. The average Briton moves house eight times in their lifetime, according to a statistic found on Google. So what I am going to do is now chart my homes, through my life, with my memories of those places.

But, as a preamble, I was always fascinated by the fact that my parents slept in the Bois De Boulogne, having missed their train, on the way home to London from Trieste one time, when my mother was carrying me, pregnant. Whatever my mother had been feeling in trepidation, vulnerable, had, I surmised, communicated itself to me in my embryonic state, leaving me incapable of feeling at home for the duration. Forever really. A sort of nomad. But I have been sedentary for 20 years now.

My mother had a hard birth. She was small, petite, dark-haired. She had commented to the midwife that finally the pains had lessened, which occasioned the midwife to press down on her and finally get me out.

My first months were, I think, passed in the house of my grandparents. This was a three-bedroomed semi-detached built possibly in the forties, perhaps even thirties, with a bay window in the lounge, a large tree in the front garden and an adequate back garden, with two fruit trees. The rooms were of pleasing proportions, with a large bathroom upstairs, and a toilet under the stairs on the ground floor.

Across the road were other similar houses, built slightly later. Out the back there were playing fields. I remember the stretch of green grass, even if I don't recall anybody playing on it! My grandparents lived there for the following fifteen years, until my grandmother passed away. Down the road were some Nissen huts, used for the army during the war and which would eventually be replaced by more housing.

Next door, I recall a jovial neighbour. Her name was Rusty, or was it a nickname, as she had the most gorgeous red hair? Opposite was a family with a couple of daughters, with whom I played. And down the road, a future colleague at school, in some houses built later.

My paternal grandmother suffered a collapse of her spine and spent years in bed, tended by my grandfather. We would visit them each weekend. Before she had got so ill, my parents took advantage and left me with them Saturday nights. I was usually happy with this.

My grandmother had been a school secretary and she had wished to have been a teacher, but her family circumstances had not permitted her further education. However, the teacherly instinct worked its way out by her teaching me mental arithmetic and giving me spelling tests. I really liked these activities, they were like games for me: Sunday mornings spent in bed for half an hour with a couple of little tests. My spelling has always been good and this must be attributed to those early 'games'. Also my ex-husband tells me he is impressed by my mental arithmetic even now. These things were gifts to me from my grandmother, whom I called Nonna.

The tending by my grandfather of my grandmother impressed my son, as he realised that the ethos of care seems to be strong in our family. Certainly, when my mother later broke her hip and ended up sleeping in the lounge, my father slept on the floor beside her, and even young Leo, about eleven years old at the time, spent one night on the floor beside her. The health visitor commented that we seemed to be caring a lot and compared us to the sort of care she found in Asian families.

My grandma's sister died young in the Spanish flu outbreak of 1918, which swept across Europe. Her name was Naomi, but I don't know where she was buried.

My earliest recollections of my grandfather were of him chasing me around the garden pretending to be a monster: cheeks blown out and arms outstretched, myself running around giggling. He was a quiet man, the youngest of five siblings and devoted to my grandmother, who was armchair-bound for the years that I remembered her, until the collapse of her spine (and then bed-bound). My grandfather had been a clerk in a shipping office at the Colonial and Eagle wharves and it was the occasional treat for me to go up to work with him, a trip out to London. His father had been a Thames river policeman who got the George Cross for saving someone drowning in the river, but my father would laugh and just say my great-grand-father had fallen in drunk.

Despite this disparaging cynicism, Dad had framed the certificate and the medal which my great-grandfather had earned, and these are now on the wall of my study in my current abode. The family had come from Deptford, which was a rough working class area, until it had become gentrified not so long back, my family having moved out decades earlier.

I am not sure which side of the family was John Crampton, my grandpa's dad, or granddad, I suppose. He and his brother were agricultural labourers who lived in Headcorn and who married two young sisters from Staplehurst, country folk.

My father, around the time of my birth, had been lucky enough to put down a deposit on a house that was being built. It cost £3,000, he told me subsequently, when that sum seemed derisory. At that time he was a clerk in central London, a job that he hated. Apparently he had been belittled for not knowing how to spell forty and he threw the job in, a pretty brave thing to do with a young family. From that job, he started working locally, in the Central Garage, where his main task was to find retread tyres. We don't do that anymore! He stayed there for perhaps a decade, perhaps a little longer, under the aegis of one Mr. Brown.

Then the opportunity came up for him to actually purchase a garage as a going concern and here he recruited a partner, a Mr. Smith, and went into business on his own account. I remember my father worked himself sick, and basically worked himself into the ground. But it was at a time when cars sold, so he was on the up.

The house Dad purchased was also a three-bedroomed semi-detached. It was in a road called West Hallowes. We were halfway up the hill, with a roundabout at the top. My father said he had never really felt at ease there. We were on land which had originally belonged to Eltham Palace, and there was a story that the gallows were up at the top of the hill. Perhaps Dad had made that up to explain away a feeling.

At any rate, I spent my first 16 years in that house. My father, tall, blonde and willowy, had dug a pond in the back garden. While he was doing that I was apparently, to the horror of the neighbour, picking up snails and eating them. Age three. The pond was a success. It had a black plastic skin, and was filled with the appropriate weed to keep the water clear and there were goldfish in it.

The back garden was great. There was a raised section in which there were fruit trees: a cherry and a pear, also blackcurrant bushes. There was a greengage tree, which was the source of my love of that fruit, and a section where vegetables were grown. The earth, virgin, was very fertile. There was also a grass section in the middle, a lawn to picnic on. By the front door, my mother had planted a wisteria. In the fifties, milk was still delivered by horse and cart and my mother would assiduously go and pick up the horse manure and spread it around the wisteria, which grew big and strong.

The lounge overlooked the street, the hill. There was a Rediffusion radiogram, which was more or less a prize possession. My mother would listen to *Music While you Work* (which I always thought was 'Music waylee work') when hoovering. There was also a small selection of records, Tchaikovsky's Concerto Number One, Borodin's Polovtsian Dances, Guy Mitchell 'Singing the Blues', Perry Como, 'Catch a Falling Star' and 'Volare'. This was about it until I started buying records in my early teens, with possibly The Beatles' *Abbey Road* as one of my first purchases. I soon developed a predilection for jazz and Ella Fitzgerald joined the collection.

One day I woke up and looked out of my bedroom window, which was the small single bedroom overlooking the street, to see that the road was all a brilliant yellow. It had been tarred and then covered with yellow shingle or gravel. It looked like a strip of sand. There was a sense of wonder at its brightness, I still recall this now.

My next door neighbour became quickly my best friend. Our birthdays were just one week apart and we spent most of our spare time together, playing with dolls or, later, out on our skates or our bikes. We raced down the hill on sleds made of two sets of roller skates strapped together, or swooped down on our bikes, slipping on the bright yellow gravel and having accidents. We wandered around 'the block', with stern warnings not to go any further. We were, anyway, hemmed in by the A20, along which the cars would thunder, speeding. It was said motorbikes would try and hit 100 mph up there, in the time before speed limits.

Up the road were two more girls, slightly older than us, and best friends themselves too. We would form a little group and play together, but they seemed more serious, older as they were.

In the very cold winter of 1963 we had central heating put in. For days and weeks this necessitated holes being created in the walls, with snow blowing in. Until then, changing for bed in the winter meant coming down in front of the lit fire in the lounge and changing there, with heat on the chest and cold on the back. Frost froze on the inside of the windows in winter, but finally we would be warm.

There was never a sense of community in that street, although we knew most of the neighbours. Across the road was an old woman, distinctly curmudgeonly. Up the road, another young girl, whose family were the first to get a television. Directly opposite was a detective and his family, the wife always sweet and smiling.

Next door to the left were a great Cockney couple, whose daughter, Phyllis, had married an American airman and had gone to live in America. Down the road there was another family with two girls who we became friends with and next door to them a family, the man an American, a daughter adopted and a son. Next door but one, next to the Cockneys, was a couple with a young son. I don't think that in all those 16 years we were there he ever acknowledged me and my mate, said hullo, nothing, passing by in sullen silence, symptomatic of suburban anomie. Houses in that road were selling at half a million in 2017.

My parents, however, had a small coterie of friends who were very close and whom we would see most weekends. The couples also had a variety of children: three in one family and four in the other. We were all around the same age, and I have very pleasant memories of days out picnicking, either in the woods and fields, walking in the autumn and going to the beach in the summer, the ninety-minute drive down to Bexhill-on-Sea, with the hot and steamy traffic jam on the way back.

For me, the children of these couples were like cousins, our being together so frequent, and their parents stand-ins for uncles and aunts I did not have in UK. There was never any associating with the parents of my neighbour. I don't know why. There seemed to be some unexplained attrition which I could only just put down to anti-Italian feeling. Who knows now, the persons long dead. Dad mentioned some person he was working with in the office, who had insulted my mother. On a drunken trip home on the train, he had had to push the man's head out of the window as he vomited: a charming image of a sick racist.

And then there were the dogs. From early on my parents had a dachshund. Her name was LoobyLoo, after the ragdoll in *The Flower Pot Men*. Really? She was a tough dog and bore two clutches of puppies. In the first litter LoobyLoo had seven puppies but one died. In the second litter, she gave birth to ten puppies and with some help from my parents, feeding the runt, the entire litter survived. LoobyLoo was definitely a good mother. Protecting her pups, she bit me when I put my hand in her kennel to stroke her!

So, years later, I was told that porn stars use a formula for finding a name. Mine would have been LoobyLoo Hallowes: the name of a pet plus the name of one's first abode!

In my early teens, as we were precocious at that time, the early sixties, the friendship with the neighbour was displaced by a boyfriend. I don't recall much of living in that street, a sort of alienation, everybody closed off, but the boyfriend took me into a world of spoilt public school pupils, misogynistic and cruel, the world of Lynn Barber's *An Education*, where husbands would cheat on their wives if they could. The boyfriend was a philanderer. However, he married, eventually, the next girl after he went out with me, when I tired of his flirting and unfaithfulness. He carried on the philandering, eventually throwing himself off a fifth-floor hotel balcony as the girlfriend of the time threatened to alert his wife. This was an unrelenting tragedy as he had been a cross-country runner, and was now, having survived, relegated to a wheelchair.

I don't recall being lightheartedly happy. My parents rowed a lot. There would be a month or two of peace and then tensions would build up and there would be a massive volcano of a row. Christmases were hard. My father was an alcoholic and would come home having started drinking in the afternoon at work. Christmas would inevitably be the time of a particularly virulent quarrel, once leading to a black eye for my mother. They were rowing up in my bedroom and my father lashed out. In response I went up to the church to get a bit of peace, but the doors were locked.

The aggression wasn't only directed to my mother. On a couple of occasions Dad arrived home a great deal the worse for wear after having fought with people he had met in pubs. One time he said he had fallen over a wall, to explain the rips and blood on a blue silk suit he had had made in Thailand on a trip.

There was, however, a leisure/pleasure aspect to Dad's drinking. It has to be said that all his friends drank a lot. They had frequent parties through the summer, and my father would suddenly pack my mother in the car and drive off at midnight, down country lanes – no motorway then – to Bexhill to have a midnight swim. He would then drive back and complete a day's work. He was made of stern stuff.

Then, as if there wasn't enough with continuously decorating and redecorating the house, there were the boats. At some stage in my early teens, Dad decided to buy a boat. The first one was some ancient metal affair called the *Stella*, which I recall stank of must. This meant that weekends were spent driving down to Ramsgate, where the boat was moored, for endless diy-ing on the boat. Eventually he bought an echo-sounder and got this renovated with six berths. Mum and Dad would then cross the Channel with my grandfather in tow, as now my nonna had passed away.

Once a week, on an evening, they would go down to Greenwich, to the *Cutty Sark*, where they learnt navigating at classes, rather successfully, I would say. There was one cross-Channel trip, however, when we got stuck in fog and I recall Mum rather humorously out in the stern of the boat with a bell, trying to alert any cross-Channel traffic.

These weekends were just excuses for a lot more drinking. Going across to Calais meant buying booze duty-free. Once out of port – was it three miles out? – they were allowed to open the drink they had bought. We met some curious people: a Cockney who had made money in fish and chip shops and knew the infamous Krays. Another who got caught with a hold full of Pakistanis trying to make it into the UK. He must have gone to jail. I don't recall.

Later in his life my father mellowed and I wonder now how he would cope with his own aggression and then his quiet and posed demeanour when he was sober. There was, however, a stolid and ethical base to his character. On one European holiday to the Canary Isles, he had saved the life of a German tourist who was floundering in heavy waters. My father was a strong swimmer, and had won several cups for this while in the army.

Generally speaking those drunken occasions were hidden under a veneer of middle-class respectability, but it was known he was a drunkard. It is difficult, however, to ponder on this and then on the man who was contemporaneously a devoted father and essential to me, someone who took pride in me and encouraged me on. He saved my life. He was a rock and a sanctum for myself and my two boys later on.

Perhaps this alcoholism was self-therapy for depression and perhaps this was one of the inherited factors which fed into my own instability. Is there a link, a gene? I don't know why I focus on this bad behaviour of my father now. Perhaps I found it frightening, the weft and weave of my childhood pulled apart, the structure of family rattled. When my father died, I cried more than I had ever cried in my life, my face feeling stiff from the tears, like a wooden mask.

Apart from that, were we a normal family? I do believe my mother, Italian, and visibly not English, suffered anti-Latin racism, for the Italians were in the war against the British. My son reiterates that he suffered racist jibes when at school, usually along the lines that the Italians lost the war, a strange sort of comment, since the boys had not known war.

My mother was far from her family and her own mother died before she had the chance to go and see her. But certainly leaving my grandmother had a strong effect on Mum. A counsellor I went to later on suggested that my mother's grieving may well have had an effect on me in my youth, passing on anxiety.

My maternal grandparents were more or less unknown to me. I don't recall Nonna Gemma at all. She had died in her fifties from a weak heart, brought on when my uncle, then young, came home very late one day during the Bora, the strong wind that blows up the Adriatic to Trieste. He felt guilty for her death right into his later years, a confession he made to me over one boozy dinner in Trieste in the nineties.

My maternal grandfather was a dapper man, always smartly dressed, his name attesting to his Catholicism: *Sperandio* (hope in God). Earlier on he had been a shop steward in the unions, when he worked on the ships, for the Lloyd Triestino. During the war he had been taken down to Sicily and the story went that he walked the entire length of Italy when he managed to free himself from capture, surprising my grandmother by turning up dishevelled and lice-ridden from his thousand-mile walk. My mother told me that Nonna Gemma would attend séances, to try and divine when and how he might get back.

I recall a visit he made to the UK. He had brought me a toy he had made himself, a horse jumping on a little trolley. I remember having chocolate spread sandwiches one day when we went up with him to the Natural History Museum. And I recall him being ill, cancer, and my being told to leave him to sleep as he was at my aunt's house, the year of his demise eluding me. He had decided not to have any operation for the cancer as he had thought this would just prolong his suffering, a different world in the fifties.

It was said that my mother and father wanted more children, but isn't the lack of vitamin D from sunshine sometimes blamed for women's infertility? A snippet heard somewhere. So I guess I was a spoilt child, although my father denied this. I can remember being a pain for my mother in my early teenage years, though. Female rivalry perhaps.

Summer holidays were a big thing in my childhood, however. We could not afford to go to Italy each summer, so Dad saved up for two years, my mother earning pennies, pin-money from mending silk stockings (not the throw-away we are now used to) and our trips were biennial, by car, flights too expensive for the ordinary person then. Difficult to conceive, in these days of cheap flights, that three days on the road could be cheaper.

Travel was pilgrimages to the town of my mother's birth: Trieste. We drove down seemingly endless avenues of plane trees in France, with hypnotic dazzling light. When we saw another car on the empty roads we waved. If the car was English, we stopped and swapped notes. Over the mountains, cars stopped at the high passes, no tunnels then, their radiators boiling over. I would hide my head under a cushion, frightened of the great drops next to the roads.

One summer, on arrival in Trieste and being overwhelmed by the sea sparkling blue, with the fairytale Miramare Castle white in the sunshine, the rugged cliffs rearing up behind, I burst into tears. Nonplussed, my parents asked what was wrong. I said I didn't want to leave. 'But you are only just arriving' they laughed. I loved Trieste, not just for its beauty but also for the warmth of my mother's relatives, adoring aunts, numerous cousins, of whom one was a renowned dialect actress who featured in Fellini's *La Città delle Donne*, a vivacious young uncle, Claudio, who swept me away on his Lambretta around town, later young cousins. Leaving Italy was, however, always accompanied by tears for me and I retained a sense of home being Trieste: that home where the heart got lost. I dreamt constantly of going to live in Italy. One day I would.

Soon I would be able to travel alone and my parents sent me in three years consecutively to Trieste, where my adored uncle and aunt would give me hospitality. At this time, I would go down to a particular beach establishment and I made friends with a gang of young people who went there regularly. We would be out on the beach till eight in the evening, often going off in dinghies to nab some mussels and eat on the beach. Some members of this gang remained friends for many years, even after I had been to Ethiopia and back. One, like an older sister for me, was even instrumental in getting me a job in Trieste later on.

My schooling was fairly routine and standard, but it was good. I went to a little infant school up the road. Then to a primary school, one station down the suburban commuter line: no drives to school at that time, all public transport. When I went on to secondary school, the local girls' grammar, it was a walk and a bus ride and then another walk down the hill, the eponymous Eltham Hill. In the summer I would walk back across fields, but always aware that there might be some threat lurking, the odd flasher.

One day my parents moved. All I had to do was walk out of West Hallowes in the morning and walk back into West Park in the evening, again possibly a perimeter of the Eltham Palace grounds. This was the second of my homes, and a discernible difference in class and style.

Chapter Two

Moving on

So, moving from my first home to my second was just walking out the door of one and back into the other house. This was a large Victorian semi-detached with a Virginia creeper all over the front. My kitchen at home now sports a biro-drawn signed depiction of this, done by someone I don't know, a gift for my parents. The moving was an upward trajectory in more ways than one. The neighbours here were one notch up the rungs of the middle classes, a woman who was one of the first to get a degree, Welsh, curious, intellectual, a writer. Mabel Blattner had written a three volume history on the context of the Bible. It is still on my shelves now and I have referred to it to see what she had to say about the great flood. Mabel would have prolonged discussions about politics with my father. On the other side, there was the bank manager and his four children, and, after they moved, a lecturer in Classics.

We had moved up in the world, from the fifties semi, to this semi, around the corner, in a long avenue of impressive tall horse chestnuts. West Park, also redolent of the park of Eltham Palace.

Meanwhile I have to thank far-sighted teachers at the grammar school for girls for steps which altered the course of my life further. Classes in disciplines were taught by different teachers at secondary, no longer all subjects taught by one class master or mistress. The teachers were generally amiable, and although drugs got into the school in the sixties, the main misbehaviour was early and presumably unwanted pregnancies, partly due to fairly ineffectual sex education. In fact the sex education, as I recall it, was hopeless.

There was, however, the school ogre. To our chagrin, on our return from summer holiday in the fourth year, who should walk in but the terrifying Miss Kennedy. A tall, grey-haired and stern spinster, she was, nonetheless, a good teacher. She was instrumental in the first of the big steps on my path through education. She was both our form teacher and our English teacher at that time. She set a fairly routine essay title for one of our first homeworks: a childhood memory.

I wrote about Trieste. I recalled that my great aunt had an Alsatian dog that was chained up outside the house, but was friendly. I recalled that I was so small, the dog towered over me even sitting. When Miss Kennedy got hold of this essay, she hauled me up to talk to her. Is my mother Italian? Yes. Do I speak Italian? No. So the mother got hauled up by the teacher too. Teach your daughter Italian was the order! There was no Italian tuition at the school, but my mother had been trained in the *Magistrali* in Trieste and had a teaching diploma, so she was fit to teach me grammar (she was very proud of this qualification). I was allocated time at home to study this. I took General Certificate of Education (GCE) Ordinary (O) level and when it came to going into the 6th form, I opted for Italian again (along with French and Spanish).

At this point my mother was not up for teaching the literature which was required, so Miss Kennedy found another teacher in some London suburb - Holland Park, I think - a long way away, who could teach me literature. Fortunately we had an extremely assiduous French teacher who taught us how to structure and write essays, so I was able to apply this to my Italian, as I seem to recall that my Italian lessons weren't that frequent. When it came to the exams, it was a long hot summer and I could take my work into the garden and sit peacefully and study, setting a table and chair out under the trees, such a lovely leafy garden.

So, another house. I lived there for two years, and then went to university: again, prompted by a foresighted teacher. This was the Latin teacher, who had become our form teacher. She almost kicked me out of the class because I used to sit and chat all through her lessons, but I begged her to let me stay, because at that time, you couldn't study Modern European languages at university without Latin.

I think I failed the O level mock, but I scraped through the actual exam with an E. I did not think I wanted to go to university at all, but this teacher, whose name is lost to me now, persuaded me to apply: I could refuse an offer, but if I didn't apply and changed my mind in the other direction, I would have to wait another year. When I got my A level results, I attained two As and a B, and our neighbour, Mabel, the lady with a degree, opined that I should apply for Oxford or Cambridge. Since that would entail waiting another year and doing an entrance exam it didn't seem to be an option; and anyway, I didn't feel that I was material for those prestigious universities - though what a difference to my life that would have made, albeit *how* is obviously not clear. I wonder now whether I would have had a breakdown earlier on in my life had I been under the social pressures of Oxbridge.

My father, who had not been to university, indeed, he had left school at 15, was very proud and supportive of my continuing to study. My mother, instead, felt that opening the doors to knowledge would just create anxieties, that a traditional role would be more likely to foster happiness. Why this should be so is paradoxical, as my mother herself had a diploma permitting her to teach and had also commenced courses at Venice's famous *Ca' Foscari* before the war put an end to her studying. Also, as we shall see, mental hospitals are full of women whose relationships have broken down drastically.

When I got the results from these exams, I was in Trieste for the summer with my aunt and uncle. I thought the examination board had made a mistake and kept waiting for a letter of apology to say that I had not got those marks.

There was a boyfriend in the offing. While I was away, he had asked my father if he could marry me. My parents were taken by surprise and gently pointed out that they didn't think I would want to get married. When I returned I was surprised too. And I didn't want to get married, but neither did I really want to let go of the boyfriend. 'If he loves you, he will wait for you,' my mother said. He did. But after four years at university I had moved on and only wanted my hedonistic freedom. Actually I was ready to flee the suburbs completely.

I lived in the house in West Park for two years, but never really went back there to live after university. It was a house I loved, though, with large well-proportioned rooms, an open stairwell, with an elegant staircase, and four spacious bedrooms, one which would accommodate my grandfather when Nonna passed away. My own bedroom was under the eaves, with a view of the garden. There was a small conservatory at the back of the house, with a built-in bar for my father.

At Leeds University I did a four-year course, a BA Honours in Modern Languages, and I wanted to do this in order to get a year away in Italy. As fate would have it, rather than go to Italy for the year, I went to France.

Home, then, in my early years, was composed of these two houses, in suburban south-east London. There is a divergence in language in the sense of home in Italian and in English. In the latter, home is most commonly a house, although it could also be a houseboat, or a bungalow, a flat. In Italian, *casa* is just the word for house and often does not have the weight of the hearth, we have in English. Hearth in Italian is *focolare* and is almost visibly the place where the fire burns, the fireplace.

Given that the British move more than the Italians, this lighter weight on the notion of *casa* is almost paradoxical. Now that I think about it, I don't recall my Italian mother ever suggesting to me that we go home. Oddly, because she was a great homemaker. Indeed, both parents were always decorating and doing up the house, never still. My mother hoovered every day, a slave to housework. My father was out. A routine existence, despite some tendency to flare up, as Grayson Perry said years down the line, 'the average family: depression, mental illness, alcoholism and abuse'.

Chapter Three

Going away, first travels

My first week at university was one of the most trying I had experienced. I was a long way from home. It was the North, a culturally different beast from London. I wasn't sure I wanted to study more. The blessing was that I found myself in lodgings with a young woman who became and still is a firm friend. Humorous and pacific, she was a godsend. We could have fought or just not got on, but we didn't (fight -we *did* get on!).

Notwithstanding this, I have memories of being shepherded around the university campus at Leeds, dejected, in Freshers' week on misty, nay foggy, dark autumn nights, waiting for the next activity before embarking on the journey home, which entailed two bus-rides and took quite a while, forty minutes or thereabouts. You could never see the horizon in those days, for the industrial smog, but gradually over the four years I was in Leeds, with the Clean Air Acts the atmosphere cleared.

The lodgings were the property of a spinster and her brother, and we would often go home and dine with her, paying her a fee over and beyond the stipulated rent, which was for bed and breakfast. There was never any attrition, the landlady was a sweet person. The boyfriend was still in the background, but eventually faded as new friends came onto the scene. One of these was the convenor of the fencing club, as, influenced by my flat-mate, I joined the fencing society. That didn't last long. Fencing was not to be my forte.

The next four years of my life were devoted to the academic study of French and Italian, with Fine Art in the first year. For the second year, and then onwards, my housemate and I found a place to rent nearer to the university, and enlisted three more young women to come and join us. These were terraced houses, with five bedrooms that landlords crammed students into.

The first thing I did when I moved in was paint a wall a dark ultramarine, (a colour I would later also use in my house in Addis Ababa). It was a sociable and enjoyable existence, and we did get some studying done. I would say I was happy in the house we shared accruing sisters I had never had.

It was not common for students to have cars at that time, but because my father was in the business, I was given a car for my eighteenth birthday. This was a little grey Fiat 500, and I learnt to double declutch. Does anybody do that anymore? One of the trips I took with two of my housemates was up to the North York Moors. It snowed. I don't recall being the slightest bit fazed about driving over steep hills in the snow, but it must have been a skiddy session.

Part of the degree course was to spend time in the country of the language studied. I had wanted to go to Italy for a year, but the French department was much better organised and they found me a place as a language teacher in a French school.

During the year in France, I acquired a handsome lover. Michel was a charming, mop-headed, tall, gangly teacher of special needs kids at the partner boys' school, who had a hobby of photography. When he returned with me to the Victorian semi, he set up a dark room at the top of the house and revivified the photography developing equipment that had been my parents', as they had the same hobby when I was a baby.

The boyfriend took me skiing in the winter, and come spring we headed off down south to Nîmes and Arles, to St. Tropez, La Grande Motte, the Camargue. It was a whistle-stop tour and it was brilliant. We had travelled down via Beaujolais, Provence and Haute Provence and he recounted the lurid tale of a young couple and their daughter who had been murdered by farmers in the village of Lurs. I was nervous about camping. This increased that anxiety! Meanwhile the scenery and landscapes were beautiful, some rugged and exotic.

The work at the school was stimulating and the pupils, at the girls' school, were all extremely disciplined and variously interested in learning English. There were school trips to the theatre in nearby Lyon, and I recall I saw the entire *Ring* cycle by Wagner. I also joined a choir. My accommodation during that year was in the attic of the annexe of the girls' school, bare but perfectly adequate. The English teaching staff were friendly and hospitable.

One of the more interesting things I recall from that year was having been invited to act as interpreter for a journalist from *The Scotsman*. He had come over to Bourgoin-Jallieu to report on the projected new town which was going to be built there. It was. Now called L'Île d'Abeau, it was a spill-over town for Lyon. At the point when I was interpreting, there was nothing there bar fields. In 2016 it had a population of 16,427 people!

The house in Leeds, meanwhile, kept a room for me when I came back. I had also been to Italy for a term, had lived in Brescia while teaching English there and then gone to Trieste to find again my friends from the beach. These were the same group of friends I had known now for three years or so.

It is only really as I write this now that I realise what an itinerant existence it was for those four years, with just months spent in any one house. I suppose the reason not to feel giddy about it was that this experience was shared by all those other thousands of students. By the time I had finished my course in Leeds, however, it felt like home and I didn't want to leave, but leave I did, returning temporarily to West Park for the summer while I looked for work. Teaching.

I got a job for a couple of months just down the road in a little private school for the teaching of English. This was beginning to be big business. Here there were pupils from a wide range of countries, but I recall a big group of Japanese girls, assiduous and keen learners.

In the endeavour to find a job after university - I wasn't going to stay teaching in a London suburb! - I had again been influenced by a teacher at school, some six years earlier. In an English lesson, we were all asked which newspapers we read. My parents at that time used to get the *Daily Express* whose only virtue, as I could see, was Giles the cartoonist. Egged on by the teacher, Miss Thompson, I got the delivery converted to *The Times*.

I don't recall ever reading the news, but when it came to looking for jobs, I combed the 'Personal' column. There were various teaching jobs advertised in Spain, Russia and Italy, my chance to fulfil a dream of living there, but ultimately I applied for a job in Ethiopia: 'governess'. My main impetus at that time was to get as far away as possible.

Chapter Four

Africa

The interview took place in Oxford. Ostensibly I was replacing a UNA volunteer who had come back to the UK for personal reasons. The job, I thought, was to teach English to a family of orphaned Oromo children, who had been adopted by a Danish forestry expert, working for the Swedish Aid Agency, SIDA, at a sort of permanent encampment, called the Chilalu Agricultural Development Unit, CADU, in Asela. I knew nothing about Ethiopia, although on the television at that time there had been a documentary called *The Hidden Empire*, which looked at the churches (you can now find this on YouTube). In the 1960s and 70s it was considered a mysterious land, a high plateau with precipitous mountain ranges and a sparse population.

I got the job, and in September, prepared to depart, collecting a few books which I would use to teach, and with one large suitcase of clothes, several miniskirts, I recall. The flight was about eight hours, through the night. After dawn we passed over desert and scenery from the moon: huge gorges, gouged into red volcanic earth. Near habitation one could see from the plane, as we stopped over at Asmara, the astounding terraces, facilitating agriculture.

Approaching Addis Ababa, the land was green, it had just rained. One could see the compounds with the round mud huts and a mass of yellow. This was Maskal flowers, which bloomed at this time of year, Ethiopian Christmas, Timkat, and usually after the long rains. It looked enchanting, diverse, different, captivating. We landed, and I was greeted by my employer of that time, Gunnar Poulsen. Holding his hand was the youngest of the children I would be teaching, Bulbulla, a wily little guy who seemed relatively shy to begin with. Most characteristic was that particular scent of the tropics, sun-baked earth.

We headed off out of the capital towards Asela, stopping at Nazret, or Adama, where Bulbulla's two little sisters, Masha and Etiye, were at a school run by nuns. We may have met also Bulbulla's oldest brother, Hirpo, who was working as a mechanic, and who kept an eye on the little girls, alone in their school. The road took us down through the Rift Valley, with its very large mountains, a long way away, and then back up along the slopes of Mount Chilalu, to Asela, the part of the road from Adama to Asela not paved. When the drought occurred a few months later, the valley was swathed in a thick smog of dust blown up from the dry land.

We passed through the little provincial capital, all on dirt roads at that time, with its shops, all mud with corrugated iron roofs, and out, onward. The Development Unit had a stretch of asphalt road, past its offices, and then further down, houses made of brick, all looking down with a magnificent view over the Rift Valley, to Lake Abaya. The houses were inhabited by the Swedish 'experts' and the Ethiopian heads of departments.

We arrived to be greeted by the rest of the household, Bulbulla's sister, Gobaneh, their two brothers, Tibeso and Melkeso and a young wife. There lies another story. Gunnar Poulsen had come to hear of a young woman who was being inveigled into an arranged marriage against her will. And as you do, he decided to abduct her. If she spent a night out with him, she would be unfit for the arranged suitor and Gunnar could marry her. Which he did. It wasn't a brilliantly happy arrangement, for the young wife, Kuni, seemed unhappy anyway. She would be part of the little class that I would be teaching.

Meanwhile, I found that my residential quarters were a perfectly adequate mud hut with corrugated iron roof in the back garden, next door to the sleeping quarters of Bulbulla and Tibeso, and the classroom.

That first evening we went out for a walk, up through the plantation that Gunnar had been tending. Then I started to feel really dizzy. The altitude: we were at about 2,000 metres and I was unaccustomed to this. A good night's sleep put me back into fine fettle. On the occasions I went into the small town with the family, young children would run behind shouting '*ye dimmet eyn, ye faras tzagur*' at my blue cat's eyes and long straight horse's hair, different from theirs.

Gunnar had high hopes for his children. Why not? I was not there just to teach English, but we had textbooks for history, geography and maths. Gunnar would come up to me and ask me to teach about why the stars are in the sky? Could I teach Tibeso to type? He had an idea of me as some sort of Renaissance woman, with all sorts of facts, science, arts, at my fingertips. We plodded along.

I think one of the most successful things I did with the children was make some sandals. We had been in Addis Ababa, to the market, and Melkeso chose a skin, out of which we cut shapes and made ourselves some flipflops. This was a flight of enterprise on my part, and, surprisingly, very successful.

I made friends with some of the young professionals there, the Swedish experts, and a couple of engineers. After my mornings with the children, I would read in the afternoon, or we would go out walking, or riding with the family. There was also some work in proof-reading articles for publication concerning agricultural development. In the evening, I would meet up with the guys, for evenings of boozy conversation and argument. Ideas of development and how to go about it were never far from discussion.

I made some good friends there. One of the guys later visited London and was racially abused in the street, something which made me feel utterly ashamed for my chavish compatriots. The same friend set up a business in Nairobi and I would see him regularly there when I went later on.

After a year, Gunnar had accepted employment in Tanzania and would take the family away from their home. Meanwhile, I had met the geographer Geoffrey Last and his family and they were able to find me work in Addis. They also provided me with hospitality in their large rambling (mud) house in the centre of town, until I met some young volunteers, who had a space in a smaller house at the other end of town, mud huts all.

I was employed in the Antiquities Administration, which would later become the Ministry of Culture. Part of my duties was to translate items from French to English, as the Institute of Archaeology received aid from the French. Also, the Government had received funds to publish the *Proceedings of the Seventh Panafrican Congress on Prehistory and Quaternary Studies,* which involved a lot of proof-reading and liaison with the printers: my job, under the tutelage of the late great Africanist scholar Dr Berhanou Abebe, who would later become a lecturer in history at the University (I discovered this years later when I was living in Italy and saw him on the TV), as well as an esteemed member of various international councils.

Jonathan Dean in his 2017 book *I Must Belong Somewhere*, writes 'The world now moves with a pace that means it is harder or indeed pointless to put down roots. You can feel at home anywhere.' His statement is linked to the omnipresence of technology and technological means of communication, but my experience in Ethiopia predated this plurality. You couldn't phone Ethiopia without an operator connection at that time, and I recall ruefully receiving my first telephone call from my father, as I had thought I had run away from him.

On the other hand, our various trips out of Asela – up a couple of mountains on horseback – or out of Addis Ababa, down rough tracks around southern and eastern Ethiopia, were carried out without the possibility of phoning anyone up should there be a breakdown. Our means of transport were in no way gleaming new vehicles. The people I travelled with would have been able to fix most breakdowns.

It was surprising how people materialised out of a landscape where there seemed to be no-one, and many of these – boys usually - also had some rudimentary and phenomenally enter-prising skills at mending and patching. One visit I made to Asela when I was living in Addis in my very old Volkswagen Beetle, saw the brakes fuse, but one of my passengers was adequately handy with a screwdriver to unblock the problem, at least until we got back into the capital: we were down in Adama. There were always peasants walking along the road. One time I saw a body at the side of the road, naked, bloated, robbed: the bus didn't stop for him.

I don't know whether I put down roots in Ethiopia. Years later an Ethiopian at a party commented I had picked up Ethiopian body language. I felt at home, and because I was there at an impressionable age, the experience left me deeply scarred. The poverty was atrocious: one of the poorest countries in the world, visited by one from the richest half dozen.

Even in the more temperate climes of Addis Ababa, some people only had one set of clothes and these were often full of holes. Sundays, the then pretender would take me out to lunch. I would drink too much and end up crying in frustration and powerlessness at this dearth of well-being and comfort of others. How to change the world? Tears don't do it.

It was a character-forming experience. The texture of life was interesting and stimulating. I met many of the great palaeontologists while working at the Institute of Archaeology, and went and viewed Jean Chavaillon's dig one Christmas day. That must have been 1973. Many of these scholars were kind and talkative.

One, instead, I recall, and I know his name, treated me as if I were a moron because I didn't think palaeontology was the greatest of disciplines. Unfortunately, it was a pity I was not more interested, as Ethiopia was at the hub of discovery at that time. This was the age when 'Lucy' was found, purportedly by Don Johanson, but the voice in the Institute actually said it was one of his young Ethiopian helpers who identified the bone first.

Living with UN volunteers also meant that we were frequently hosts to young people who dropped by Addis Ababa, either volunteering or on a tour of East Africa. One of my housemates, Jamie, worked for Oxfam and journalists would drop by to glean information from him. A notable example was a *Time* journalist, who ended up writing that the children cruelly whipped each other, whereas the truth was they were playing a game like spinning tops.

Another journalist came to write about life in Addis Ababa for the *Financial Times* and sometime later I coincidentally found he had also written about Trieste, then a town little known outside the Italian borders. You couldn't imagine it.

The house had a shifting European and American lumpen-intellectual community There were three of us when I moved in, including myself. My move there had been facilitated by Judith Todd, an anthropolgist who had been staying there. She moved on and liberated a room for me. Forty years on I am still friends with my companions, now in London and Panama, and whom I contact through these wonderful technological means.

Then there was the famine. This was the first globally acknowledged and utterly desperate famine in the north of the country, which catapulted Ethiopia onto the world stage. Contemporaneously the price of wheat rocketed, as did the cost of petrol, due to moves in OPEC. The pressure on the population led to riots and slowly and stealthily the army under the command of a relatively liberal officer, whose name escapes me at the moment, performed a coup. (After 24 hours, as memory often works, his name came to me: General Aman Mikael Andom.)

My father arrived for a 'holiday' just soon after this *putsch*. Convinced that the army was not adapted to ruling, he and I would argue about the prognostications for the future. Moving around the country meant waiting at roadblocks to get out of the capital. My father was aggressively questioned at the airport as to why he was visiting the country.

For a few months events seemed to move slowly, then a further *putsch* occurred within the army itself and the liberal commander met his end, murdered. A hard-line coterie of army officials took over under Mengistu Haile Mariam, and events got tougher – well, downright bloody. A young British palaeontologist was shot whilst attempting to liaise between students and the army. My boyfriend told me I should leave. So once again the course of my life changed. The boyfriend was right, however, (as had been my father) for in the months and even years following these events, the country was in the grip of what became known as the Red Terror, with township kebbeles (committees) set up, whose frequent motivation was revenge.

The boyfriend himself very narrowly missed being executed, a tale which he told when he managed to come to England, for medical reasons, some six years later. A civil war broke out. There was a great deal of fighting, putting pressure on an already weak local peasant economy.

I left Addis Ababa in May 1975, accompanied, or rather driven by Tom, a friend in a Land Rover. The boyfriend was there to say goodbye. I still have a strong mental image of crying as I looked out of the Land Rover window, saying goodbye and him telling me not to cry.

Tom and I went down to Nairobi. The brevity of this sentence does not reflect the days driving we did to get there! Fortunately we left before the southern states were in total uproar, and our drive down through the savannahs was relatively event free.

Well. About ten miles from the Kenyan border, the gear stick broke at the root. Tom was an engineer, so he got under the vehicle and managed to wedge the gear into four-wheel drive, second gear with a rock, which enabled us to drive down to the border slowly, but surely. We were under pressure of time, because the exit visa was due to run out in a day, leaving us, were we to stay, in quite a pickle.

We made it. And at the border, past Yabelo, we were actually even luckier than we were aware of, for it had rained and the savannahs were a picture of green acacias, clear skies and astonishing views. There was a sort of moon landscape, with high termite mounds in the red volcanic earth, stunningly picturesque. This continued down through the Chaka Desert in Northern Kenya, where now the desert, a rock desert, with distant mountains, was actually in flower. Skies vibrant blue. I was later told that rainfall in that area occurred on average each six years. My friend Ahmed was later amazed by this and commented to my tutor this strange fact. I wonder what that statistic is now?

At the border, we had stayed with a Catholic priest on the Kenyan side. He had a small generator and with this, Tom was able to solder the gear stick back in place. It held right through its marathon journey over into India, and back through Afghanistan and Iran and Europe, back to Bath. Tom met his family, but I meanwhile flew back to the UK.

The story of the broken gear stick and the mission's generator became public knowledge somehow and appeared in a novel about Kenya, by Kuki Gallman, who herself was later shot in a conservation area in the country.

We stayed free in a tourist lodge, as Tom was able to offer his services in repairing some machine or other, possibly another generator. Elephants drinking at pools, palm trees, clear blue skies: as Tom commented, just think what the first European explorers made of this haunting beauty, miles and worlds away from uproar in Ethiopia.

I had a few weeks before I was due to return to England to interview for the course I had applied for. In this time, arriving in Nairobi, Tom and I met up with an archaeologist I had known in Addis, and we took off for a trip around a couple of safari parks and up to the beautiful Lamu, where I would return to study, and where now the local population of the islands, the Bajunis, have fled Al Shabaab.

More surprisingly a huge port is being built there by the Chinese. Then we went down into Tanzania: the border between Kenya and Tanzania would later close, but we were lucky. We were also lucky in spotting the peak of Kilimanjaro which is notoriously often hidden in cloud. We visited the children I had taught, who were now at the International School at Moshi and would subsequently qualify with the International Baccalaureate before moving on to Denmark, where they settled. This was pure tourism.

We camped out and watched animals. I recall visiting a village just south of the Kenya border, and being overwhelmed by the beauty of the palms inclining to a beach where dugouts took fishermen out for their provisions, people quietly going about their daily tasks. Even now I remember a delicious *chapati* I ate in a roadside café with a cup of spiced tea. How strange the memory!

We were on the road, and I felt as if I could carry on ambling around forever, and my ambition had been to come back, perhaps work for Unesco, undertake some educational post.

These were travels in places which have subsequently been convulsed by political turmoil, places of extreme poverty, where religion has arguably caused huge rifts within communities, and rebels have taken power. We were lucky and privileged to have seen quiet lives when we were there. It seems almost glib to talk of travel and tourism, while a revolution was broiling nearby.

Meanwhile I would be returning to England to study, inquiry which was to become a strong habit, and not remotely interested in settling. The idea of home didn't bother me at all.

Chapter Five

Interlude

In one of those strange coincidences that life throws at you, I had met again a man I had known at Leeds University, Phil. The go-between was a woman from London I had made friends with in Addis Ababa, Jamie's girlfriend. How complicated can it be? Housemate Jamie's girlfriend, Anita, came out to visit him in Addis and we hit it off. Subsequently, when I returned to London for a Christmas break, she had picked me up from the airport, to take me home to surprise my parents. We had bonded immediately. Anita was an ebullient character: half-Italian, like me; surname Compton, two letters away from mine; birthday just one day away - she felt like a twin.

She held a party, and Phil now working in the banking sector in the City, turned up. By some roundabout way, Anita knew him. I immediately recognised him, as he walked down the stairs into the cellar of her house, transformed into a disco. He was tall and slim with his characteristic spectacles, as he had poor sight. We got together (we got *it* together), saw each other a few times while I was still in London. We corresponded when I returned to Addis. However I decided to stay another year to renew my contract. At that point, Phil said, well okay, have a good time and the letters stopped.

Then I dreamt about him, I don't recall the dream, just that he was in it and I renewed the correspondence, suggested he come out and we travel around a bit. This shows my willingness to alter the course of my life for a dream, literally. Phil didn't come out to Ethiopia, but when I flew back to London, he was waiting. He had come round to my parents' house and was there when I woke up from a jet-lagged sleep.

The day after, June 2nd, it snowed. The day after that a heat wave set in that went on till September. That was 1975. My interview was on June 4th. It was for a Postgraduate course in Development Studies: the politics, economics and sociology of development, Bath University. Despite not having an appropriate first degree (politics, economics or sociology), I was accepted on the course on the basis of the experience I had had at CADU and in Ethiopia. All those arguments had borne fruit. Furthermore, I was to find my life experiences in the academic studies that I would later read, about the politics of coups. Really I was hankering to go back to Ethiopia, but Phil got a hold on me, and as the political situation was extremely unstable it looked unlikely I would go back. The next eight years were all involved in study and although this took me back to Kenya for fourteen months, I would paradoxically settle and find myself feeling at home in Yorkshire.

This is how it came about. When I was in Ethiopia, I had a burning desire to do something useful and Dad looked into the possibility of my studying for a degree in medicine. It would have taken seven years, and I would have had to start right from the beginning, studying science O and A levels in biology at least. I thought that was too long a period. I *did* end up being a doctor, but of something less useful and it took all those long years.

I did well at the Development Studies. Egged on by Phil,

who at that point was studying in Warwick, and a friend, I approached the tutor to suggest that I would like to do the M.Sc: this was a possibility for anybody who did well in the written exams. But the *quid pro quo* was that an M.Sc, by dissertation, should have something to do with one's first degree. So I came up with the notion of comparing French and British forms of colonialism based on the language. This would have looked at the imposition of languages, language policy in education and also on the poet Léopold Senghor's notion of *'négritude'*, that is the development of black consciousness after the decades and centuries of colonialism. The tutor looked at a proposal I had submitted. He seemed to find it interesting, but doubted I would do well enough in the written exams, and, anyway, he said, it was too big a theme for an M.Sc dissertation but could be a Ph.D. As a result of that, I started to look around to see if there was a university which would offer me a place.

As it turned out, and as suggested above, I did well enough (to the tutor's surprise) in the written exams, to pass onto higher study and a sociologist at the University of Leeds was willing to take up my theme and supervise. This was John Goldthorpe, who had written a text which became widely used in Development Studies, *The Sociology of the Third World* .

The study was premised on a period of field research. It was not possible to return to Ethiopia, so I applied to go to Tanzania. Here my proposal was turned down. So I approached the Kenyan authorities. Professor Abdulaziz at Nairobi University took an interest in my studies and offered support. Phil and I went off on holiday to Italy. When I got back, the department at Leeds phoned me to say there was a letter for me. This was the formal acceptance of my proposal: the letter had been sitting there for quite a while.

There had been two years of settled living, however. We were in a house in the countryside, built of Yorkshire stone, in Lower Wharfedale, not far from a bend in the river where we would go swimming in clement weather. This was another house of shifting inhabitants, lumpen, students. The local village was very upper middle class, with solicitors, one of whom would come down to the river with a pair of binoculars to spy on one of our inhabitants bathing nude.

The house was a tied cottage on the land of a farmer, who himself rented it from the Harewood Estate. But it felt like home. We used to grow vegetables in the garden, very successfully. I remember the first salads we grew. The growing conditions had been perfect, and the Webb's Wonders expanded to the size of large footballs. That summer I was giving away lettuces left and right and making endless lettuce soups. Emboldened by the success of this, we experimented with all sorts of other vegetables, and there was also a row of lovely gooseberry bushes, which Rick, our mentor in the field of growing (excuse the pun) had planted. There were a couple of old apple trees in the garden, but they were not particularly fruitful (oh dear!). However, by the time we had got into the swing with the gardening, I had counted 24 types of fruit, vegetables and herbs being raised. This was very satisfying. The old apple trees served to hang a hammock.

Years later I went back to see the house. It had now been bought by a man from Yorkshire TV and he had put a shed on the plot where we grew the vegetables. We chatted with him over the wall, and he said he had noticed that the soil in the garden was very rich. So, we had tended it well over the period of our living there. The house was lovely, in a beautiful and desirable location. We had been lucky to live there for a peppercorn rent.

I made new friends at the University. Over the two years of stability, in which Phil moved up to Yorkshire with me, while he was registered for Ph.D research at Warwick University, we got to know a band of Africa hands. (One of these was Tommy, who had been on the development course in Bath.) And Africans. Actually I don't really like the use of 'Africa' as a category, because it is a huge continent made up of a large variety of nations and even more peoples with hundreds of different languages. Plus, when you scratch the surface of the idea, what people really usually mean is black. My friends were South Africans, plus the English wife of one of them. We would meet up each weekend for food and drink, dancing and discussion. In addition to the informal chatter of my friends, the university was lucky to have Ralph Miliband, writer of *The State in Capitalist Society,* as professor of Politics, as well as Lionel Cliffe, who had himself been locked up in Zambia for apparently fomenting student revolt. Lionel had also set up the Centre for African Studies at Leeds and, with others, the Africanist economic journal, *The Review of African Political Economy.* The Sociology department had the renowned Zygmunt Bauman, whose seminars on culture I used to attend.

There was a lot of talking in those days. I don't know that we achieved anything, but there was a definite and sincere exchange of ideas. I don't really believe that people discuss much anymore, preferring soundbites, tweets, but perhaps events in the year 2017 have put talk back on the agenda. Who knows? Who can compare and measure it?

Looking back now it is surprising that I considered Parkview home, or rather, should I say it throws light onto what one may consider the elements of home. For instance, I spent my time with people who were not born Yorkshire people. I hankered after going away again and this expressed itself in the people I mixed with and of course the orientation of my studies. I had no family in the area, and anyway at that period of my life, I wasn't particularly interested in seeing more of the small family I did have: my poor mother and father, and an adored grandfather. When I met up with friends, we were mostly interested in politics. I don't know what good that did either, although a basic orientation to society was gained and deepened.

I am implying that one creates a community of people who come from the place inhabited, but I guess that university communities are people whose academic interests are forefronted, rather than geographical location. Certainly in Leeds, my friends were involved in the politics of development in one way or another. Whether creating a community of friends is the case now that university study is so costly and many students stay at home is a moot point. There are far more students now, more universities. University courses are shorter, in semesters and somehow the whole experience seems poorer than back in the 1970s and 80s, despite the exorbitant costs and students now saddled with loans. This as an aside.

So my studies pinged me off into the ether again, for a period of intense field research in Kenya, and when I returned my former world had moved on and things were irretrievably different.

Chapter Six

Research

My dear friend Ahmed had approached a cousin, Abdullah, who lived in Nairobi to ask for accommodation. Generously they let me into their household: Abdullah and wife Shamim, his daughter and his son Eddy. Abdullah came to the airport to pick me up and I experienced with nostalgia the strong smell of the tropical volcanic earth which had so characterised my years in Ethiopia too. But then smell is so potent as a stimulus for memory, as I had recalled from my early years going to Trieste, when it was the maritime pines which reminded me of the seaside town.

His young sister-in-law, Farida, was put at my disposition to guide me around Nairobi. The first thing I had to do was open a bank account, but I slept right through the night and into the next afternoon, so managed to miss that for the day. We lived in a University compound on the Lenana Road, which was a short bus ride from the centre of Nairobi, or a walk, perfectly doable. However I never really felt quite at home in Kenya as I had done in Ethiopia.

I embarked upon the research, having introduced myself to the Professor of Linguistics and African Languages at the University, Professor Mohamed Abdulaziz. My brief was to undertake as many interviews as I possibly could in the tourist sector. I was also permitted to tape conversations in hotels and tourist offices, with my permit from the Office of the President. It is hard to see now that this work could have been undertaken in the period of suspicion and uncertainty that has ensued in the last twenty years, but I was lucky. I managed to collect a vast amount of research material, over 100 interviews, 20 hours of tapes and about 50 questionnaires. The tapes were transcribed with the help of Kenyan students, as they included conversation in Kamba, Kikuyu, Swahili, Luo: sorry I am using the anglicized versions of these languages. But there was a rich body of transcriptions. I coined the term 'hedonocracy' for the pleasure-seeking characteristic of tourism and ultimately enjoyed collecting the research materials.

My Eritrean friend from CADU had set up an office in Nairobi and we would meet up, together with other of his friends; a small Eritrean community existed in Nairobi. So my social life was set. Other friends came from the academic community in the University, but mainly these would be other researchers, several Americans studying history I recall. A researcher studying African literature, who would take me to the trial of Ngugi Wa Thiong'o, which reached international attention, after his production of a play criticising the government.

I found, however, that relations between black and white were rather more travailed than I had been used to in Ethiopia. We got quizzical looks at the trial of Ngugi. The history of colonialism in Kenya had left scars. How surprising is that, when it was reported that areas of Mount Kenya were under air attack from the RAF in the early 1950s? When I and a friend, white, went for a drink with my Eritrean friends, black, for some reason the waiters would not serve us. For the most part, however, I was able to carry out my work with the greatest cooperation of staff and patrons in the tourist sector.

The research took me all over the country: I went down to the coast, along to Lamu. After a few months in Kenya, during which Phil came out to visit, again at Christmas, I had met another man, an Englishman (actually he was Irish) who was studying African languages, most particularly Kiswahili. I moved in with him and it was with him that I went down to Lamu to collect more information. The project enriched my research as he was able to identify some Kiswahili dialects, which had all been transcribed by students I employed to cast into text the conversations I had taped. During the time we were there, a terrible accident occurred when a ferry full of Bajunis, from the islands, capsized, killing many. This was an utter disaster, with corteges of people carrying coffins along the narrow streets. My father commented this must have had an impact on me, a sort of concertina of concern, as I saw it affected him. I can see those corteges in my mind's eye even now, with the tragedy that extended to so many families. So much grief.

Lamu was, however, for me a place of enchantment, a community which was remote from outsiders, even the Kikuyus, government officials who went down to work there. They did not seem to mix with the self-sufficient WaSwahili. Lamu had been an important trading town through the centuries, first part of the Sheikdom of Oman, but also with Portuguese traders and picturesque dhows crossing the seas to Oman. It was an island in an archipelago, with sea swirling around the other islands and mangroves, beaches of fine white sand (and sandflies).

The architecture was somewhat spectacular. Houses were

built around inner courtyards with the rooms open to capture the sea breezes. The basic construction was a wood frame blocked in with coral and with coral powder used to whitewash. The front doors were large and ornately decorated. Outside the centre of town, the characteristic mud huts with corrugated iron roofs existed. Dhows, boats with a sail, would ply their trade across the seas. One afternoon we went out on a dhow, down through and around the mangrove swamps, which grew along the island's coast.

Tourists came. There was a small hotel called Pepponi down the coast. Across the isthmus was another elite hotel. I saw a couple arrive with their cases. Tragedy hit again, as the young woman, a Japanese, drowned while diving. Paradise touched by disaster. Just because it was a holiday destination, health and safety standards should have applied.

In the hinterland to the town, there were mango orchards, and palms grew, their leaves swishing in the sea breezes. With Abdullah and his friends in Nairobi, we had humorously conjured up a research project for biologists: study the effect of the sea breeze on the growth of coconuts by the coast.

With my research brief, I was able to contact and get to know people: a wonderful young woman, Amina, who was curator of the Museum; and a man, the boss of a travel firm, who invited me to dinner at his house. This was a curious experience. I was treated extremely well, but I got to eat with the men only, and the women peered in from the kitchen, giggling. When time came to go home, I was escorted by three men down the alleys. I was also put in contact with Abdullah's wife's family, who came from the Bajuni islands, and took a trip out to visit them with an overnight stay. Unfortunately I was ill when I got there, possibly a dose of sunstroke. We had invited the curator of the Museum to dinner one evening, but I had to stay away, as I was still suffering. We never contacted a doctor: just waited for the malaise to pass. With the troubles relating to Al Shabaab, the Bajunis have now fled the area.

There was also a community of British gays there. Things ended up pretty badly for them: being gay in Kenya was, and is, punishable by long prison sentences. They must have lived under constant threat, but in those unthinking days we attributed their periodic crimes of passion to the 'murky underside of the exotic'. Some lumpen students were in Lamu: these included a blustering American, and a willowy German, studying Emin Pasha, with his American girlfriend. I have a recollection of discussions about the state of contemporary Germany, which this young man was patently fleeing. Did I feel I was fleeing, too? I had my research as my hook and anchor. Inevitably tourism was tied to both the so-called First World and the Third.

I had also spent a week or so in Malindi, down along the coast from Mombasa. Here there were many German tourists and some of them were return visitors who came back to the same hotel for as many as 15 years in a row. I also spent some time in Mombasa, interviewing and distributing my questionnaires around tour operators.

After 14 months I was due to return to the UK. I packed my research material, posted off a pile of books I had collected on various aspects of Kenyan history and society, and headed back. I was leaving the arms of one man to return to the arms of another. Which one signified 'home'? How naïve I was that I could not have foreseen the major problems that I was heading into. Also, while Kenya had been home with the scholar, the other 'home' was no longer the place of rural and bucolic peace that it had been when I left.

Chapter Seven

Breakdown

When I left for Kenya, Phil found that our friends almost inexplicably more or less abandoned him. The close coterie of Africans no longer invited him round to their parties, for reasons nobody asked about or explained and he felt a little bereft. He therefore found himself another group of friends, mainly a gaggle of younger women, to entertain him, and he also found himself another lover. For anyone reading this now, and looking in from the outside, it is obvious that problems would be brimming over on my return.

Phil had ruefully asked me when I left England for Kenya the year before whether I was going to stay faithful and I had declined. Why that should be? Itchy feet? Incapacity to stay faithful? Desires and emotions that now seem distinctly mixed and contradictory. Returning to UK Phil and I now had to accommodate our various experiences over the time I had been away and try to readjust. This was not easy. In fact, it led to a nervous breakdown on my part, a psychotic episode that would take many months to heal.

It was not just however our two personal lives which were in turmoil. The inhabitants of Parkview seemed to be at total war. A woman had moved in with one of the residents, and was working at a wholefood store with another. However, she was physically unable to shift the heavy produce and the small collective of the wholefood store had decided to ask her to leave. It fell to the Parkview resident to tell her this. Meantime she had got into several arguments with Phil. The atmosphere in the house was intolerable. Phil would go out and either come home at two in the morning, or not come in at all. When he was home, he would study till late in the night, sleeping all morning, and generally breaking my own sleep patterns. He was with Ali. I tried to be very open-minded and liberal and understanding, but the situation broke me.

In addition to the situation at home, there was a rampant sexual killer on the loose, a man who later became known as the Yorkshire Ripper. Seventeen women had been murdered and the police were calling for a curfew on women. Being out in the dark unaccompanied was frightening.

Leeds had a very lively feminist community, where there were feminists of all persuasions: radical feminists, socialist feminists, lesbian feminists. The radfems wouldn't have anything to do with men at all. In time, when they wanted children, it was known that they would choose subject men, calculate their time of fertility and ask the chosen one to oblige. A few years later, these women would have been able to benefit from *in vitro* fertilisation.

On one occasion, with the projection of the film *Dressed to Kill* the feminists went on the rampage and threw black paint all over the screen at the cinema. The media then went about trying to find the 'leader' of the feminist group, unaware at that time of the rampantly unhierarchical nature of women's groups. As a joke, they were fed the name of Betty Powers, as the leader.

Furthermore there was a strong air of liberality with a mixing of partners and casual sex the norm, amongst the University student community. Phil, in addition to now 'being with' Ali, had a bunch of groupies he spent time with, all several years younger than us.

There wasn't just this going on. My father had recently been on one of his drunken binges and thumped my poor mother, who this time said that she had had enough and that she wanted to leave him. She didn't. My sudden descent into psychosis tied her to him. This added to what was - the breakdown - a flight mechanism *par excellence*. Too much to cope with, no room for refuge.

I launched myself into another affair, just to complicate my emotions. However, it couldn't last. One day I met Phil in an emotionally highly charged state. We picked up Ali to come home with us. That evening, I looked out of the bathroom window and saw a huge mushroom cloud, a towering cumulonimbus that in my overwrought state I viewed as a nuclear holocaust, Armageddon. Phil and Ali were with me. In the middle of the night I had a dream that I had been strangled by the ripper. Apparently my scream was so bloodcurdling that I woke up the whole household. In addition, I had apparently been talking more or less incomprehensibly, although I remember even now that I was proposing a feminist theory of the emotions. In addition, since I had seen the end of the world, I was imagining that a space ship with friendly aliens was going to come down and take my friends and me away from the disaster.

The following morning Phil had arranged to get me to a doctor, with a referral to the local mental hospital. I did not know this, but was looking for the car keys to drive out, which Phil had hidden, went into the bathroom with Phil following me, then, to get away from him, turned, ran and launched myself through the bathroom window. It was on the first floor and according to Phil, when he came down, I was sitting on the grass saying 'that was a silly thing to do'. I don't recall any of this consciously at all, but the mere fact of being so out of my head certainly frightened and upset me when I was later told about it.

I was taken into the hospital, into the long-stay ward, which meant I was locked in, and treated with chlorpromazine. This sedated me to the point of total lethargy, stupor even. My friends did the trek to come out and visit, but the nurses in their 'wisdom' perceived that I was always more restless when the friends had been and simply deduced that my friends were bringing me drugs into the hospital and so banned their visits. I had never taken drugs, apart from the prescription medication the hospital put me on. No-one brought me drugs.

The long-stay ward was a tough place: we all walked around each other, steering well clear of getting near. One day I got up to find that all the women were naked in protest of something or other, sitting catatonically and smoking, as this was permitted then. Another day a small woman arrived in a tulle dress: she thought she had been shot. 'Stand on my toes, will you?' was her refrain. She wasn't in the ward long however. I don't know what happened to her.

Phil brought me in reading material: *The Magic Mountain*. He thought that being in a hospital would resonate with the tale about the sanatorium, but the book was impossibly heavy and even decades later I only managed to read about two hundred pages. My friend Ahmed brought me in V.S. Naipaul's *The Mystic Masseur*. This was lighter, but I still could not concentrate or absorb narrative. One book did chime with me, however: John Berger's *G*, winner of the Booker prize. Its episodic nature and the tale of the flight over the mountains into Milan struck a chord and I was able to start reading again. A bookish person, reading novels as well as the texts for my research, I had actually woken up thinking that I was Doris Lessing, closed into a mental hospital, like in her *Briefing for a Descent into Hell*.

Meanwhile my parents, shocked, came to visit several times, making the long drive up between London and north Leeds. My father had calmed down, my own situation being worse than whatever devils he had been fighting. The hospital was like the asylum described by Will Self in *Umbrella*, a set of Victorian towers, linked by a long tunnel, not actually under-ground but roofed over, with white tiles, like a massive public lavatory of the forties and fifties. It was a daunting place, and I was locked into it.

I didn't really seem to be getting any better. Partly I ended up feeling I was assuming the pains and travails of the other inhabitants of the ward. I think about a month of my life was spent there, before my parents organised for me to be trans-ferred – my parents were allowed to take me down – to the psychiatric unit at Orpington Hospital, just around the corner from where they were living. The first thing the psychiatrist at Orpington did when I arrived was take me off the chlorprom-azine, which had an utterly stultifying effect, and change the medication to lithium. Within a relatively short time, he was satisfied with my improvement. Whether it was the change of drug regime or the talking sessions or just time: it is not clear what helped.

However, one day, an event occurred which rather shook me. We were in a group session with several other women. In my turn, he asked me if I were going to return to a monogamous situation. I said I would not. He brusquely retorted that I would then get ill again. This shook me. Why, when I was on the way to recovery, would the psychiatrist so blatantly spell out another breakdown? One of the nurses had said to me, well done. I replied, well you could have said something to help me out. No, she said, you don't have to work with him.

I was back in Wharfedale for the bluebells. Some four months had passed between one thing and another, but I was to stay on a dose of lithium. Mainly this made me put on weight, but I felt adequately balanced. The relationship with Phil stabilised, as he broke his intimate links with Ali, remaining 'just good friends', so the psychiatrist's mantra of a monogamous relationship won out.

I got a job in the University bookshop for a few months, and when that ended, I returned to my Ph.D research and laboriously worked away at putting together a cogent narrative for the sociology and sociolinguistics of Kenya. I had had my breakdown in January of 1980. In September of 1983, I had finished and been awarded my Ph.D with Donald MacRae as the external supervisor. The night of the viva exam, I got extremely drunk on cocktails from a town bar with my internal examiner, a friend of mine, and went to an Inti Illimani concert at the town hall, where I recall walking on air. By this time, my relationship with Phil had come to an end, although we were still friends, but he had moved back to Ali.

With my Ph.D completed it now remained for me to decide what the next step would be. I itched to fulfil a dream: that of going to live in Italy. So, in late September, I set off on a tour of northern Italy, to universities where English was taught, in the hope of getting employment. My trip took me to Bologna, where a dear friend had a cousin working in the CILTA, the language centre of the University. From there I went to my beloved Trieste, and met up with an old friend from the beach days, the beautiful and charismatic Renata Caruzzi, who was now a lecturer in the Institute for Germanic Philology, the department headed by the great writer, Claudio Magris. There was, indeed, a place available, and there was a person who was after the place, but a string or two was pulled and eventually I got offered the place, as being the person with more qualifications.

That was September. I returned to Parkview and awaited news. Would I please come down by Christmas? I was asked. So I packed up house, stowed my possessions at my parents' house, which was luckily capacious, and went down to Trieste. There I would be accommodated by another of the English *lettori*. The job came through, but not without a considerable amount of strife, which would characterise the next three or four years' annual renewal of contracts. And I set about looking for my own place to live, with my father having agreed to foot the bill for a *pied-à-terre*.

It turned out that the people I was working with were fairly riotous and exceedingly good company and we would be out and about nearly every evening of the week. In addition I made some good friends who lived in Padova, and would go down the railway line to stay with them quite often. Everybody, I found, was very lively.

Then in 1985 a man walked into my life. I would say that I

fell head over heels in love with him, but thinking about him now has so little impact that I feel that the love I experienced then was illusory. For a while, about three years, we had a good time. I had by that time also found a flat, which was renovated, in the centre of town.

The lover was a teacher of Eastern European history (I Googled him just recently, and he looks seriously dishevelled and unhappy!), so we travelled down into the former Yugoslavia fairly often. In the spring we would go down to the island of Veglia, Krk, and stay over a night or two, there to enjoy the empty rocky bays. We went to Zagreb and to Belgrade, interesting experiences for me, accompanying him on lectures he gave to the universities there. He came to Geneva with me, where I visited friends and he went to do research in the United Nations library. He never came to England.

In autumn of 1987, the government delayed in renewing the contracts for the *lettori*. This preyed so much on my mind, having moved country and wanting to set up home in Italy, that I became seriously mentally unwell again. For a short while the man took care of me, then my mother came down and one evening when I went up to his house he told me he didn't love me anymore and that it was all over. I was not strong enough to take this blow, together with the problems with work, and although I sort of staggered along trying to do some work when the contracts came through, I decided that I had to leave. Run away.

Chapter Eight

Flight

Running away is never a good idea and even a psychiatrist will tell you to try and stay and work out the problem. However, throughout my life, I had usually run away, from relationships when they were getting too close, from the country, when I got itchy feet. Perhaps this was some deep insecurity, I wonder, looking back. Is wanderlust a seeking or a refuge? Had my journey to Ethiopia been a flight? Had coming back been a return? Was the motivation for the Ph.D to return to Africa, to run back again? It was.

The really silly thing about running this time, was that I had scrupulously been preparing my lessons for when the contract would come through and had material ready for many lessons. As my friend Valerie said, I could have done the job standing on my head. However I had a crisis of confidence and that was that. My mother was in Trieste with me, suffering with me, such a strain on her. But I just wanted to leave. So I took up my father's suggestion that I return to UK to heal.

It wasn't really such a good piece of advice. I had no network of friends there, and time dragged terribly. I got to a psychiatrist who pointed out that the conditions were more or less similar to the breakdown in the first instance. However I just got more and more depressed, until one day I got hold of all the pills I was taking and swallowed most of them. I blacked out. My father must have clocked what I had done. He told me he tried to make me sick. They called the ambulance, and when I awoke, I was in hospital.

Mum and Dad came in at about seven in the morning. What a night they must have had. My mother said to me it was the cruellest and most selfish thing I could possibly have done. My father, asking me what was going through my mind, was in tears. The psychiatrist said I should go into the psychiatric ward for observation. The same psychiatrist who had put me on lithium and the same hospital ward I had been in seven or eight years previously.

I don't really know what gets you well. Perhaps it is the accumulation of understanding that each person has a baggage-load of problems, some of them worse than your own. The nature of the human condition. I guess the psychiatrist changed the medication again. In Italy I had been on a cocktail of Haldol (haloperidol) with liberal dashes of Valium. What followed I don't recall. That time. Soon I was out of hospital again, and by and by went back to Trieste. Through the summer I was supposed to catch up with teaching that I had missed. In addition there was a conference on applied linguistics that I was to attend in Sicily.

Actually, it was all too soon. I went to Sicily and went out of my nut again, landing up in a small psychiatric unit in Catania. My friend who had accompanied me must have contacted my parents, because I got a phone call at the unit I was in from my mother.

For some reason, her voice came through so clear and strong that I just didn't recognise her and told the nurse, 'Questa non è mia madre', she's not my mother. How that made her feel, I can only imagine now. She came down to Sicily on her own and fished me out of the hospital, taking me to a hotel for a few nights, before we made the trip back to Trieste. I must have been quite drugged up, for I recall very little of this, bar the deep blue waters off the hotel we were staying in. I have no memory of our journey to Trieste at all, although we most probably took two flights.

When we got back to Trieste, my father flew down to be with us. He asked me if I was with the guy who had rejected me. I lied. I had gone back to him, stupidly. Very stupidly, for the guy was basically a coward. Time passed and I rockily started the new academic year, my contract renewed, my superiors having kindly kept my place open for me, ever thankful for that.

In that year following the breakdown, I would meet someone who would change my life forever. This was my husband to be. As soon as I had met him, I closed my rapport with the coward immediately.

Curiously enough my future husband's first words to me were a lie. We were at a party, and I was sitting lazily looking around when I saw him come in accompanying a friend of mine. He looked fairly ridiculous as he had a huge curly chestnut wig on. He came in the far side of a large hall where we were attending a Mardi Gras party. It certainly wasn't love at first site, and being told a lie just made me curious, but it is interesting, then and now, to note that some sort of magnetism held sway.

For my part, I was dressed as a fortune-teller, with full skirts, and beaded headscarf, complete with beauty spot marked on my face. I went to the bar and he and my friend were standing next to me. He leaned over and said to me 'I am English' with a strong accent. His next words were 'I am a businessman'. He was drunk (I wondered who was driving?) and giggling. At some stage we had a dance, everyone was up on the floor and that was it. That was the Saturday. It should be said that the Mardi Gras celebrations, even outside Venice, are pretty widespread and engrossing. The Sunday there is usually a procession in Muggia, a sort of suburb of Trieste and when I have been there it has often been extremely raw and cold. Then the final party is on the Tuesday, the actual *martedì grasso*, which is our pancake day.

So, the Tuesday after the meeting with the liar, I had been invited up to another friend's house for the big party. I have to say that I was geared up to chat up a man I had met, a doctor. However, in walked the liar, without wig. I had been standing by the door and he made a beeline for me, though he later denied this. We sat and chatted for a while, then he suggested we wander off and see what costumes and masks there were around.

We went up to another Trieste suburb, Servola, where there was a small procession of people in masks. We wandered around for a bit, then he took me home. I didn't invite him in. He invited me out for lunch the following Saturday. I was still seeing the coward. But a few evenings later, after I had started going out with the liar, I decided to go and break up definitively: possibly the best thing and the most courageous thing I had done, seeing that I thought I was madly in love with him. Now that I think about him, the blow of his leaving me and perusing over his behaviour, I feel absolutely nothing for him, while other lovers still hold a place in my heart, even though my feelings for my now-ex-husband are pervasive and intense.

Mardi Gras 1988 marked the start of another period of relative stability, which lasted for three years or so. Mauro, as my young man was called, courted me and it was a very relaxed courting.

He had a great sense of humour, something that he has not lost over the years. During this time Mauro got me back on skis, and in the winters we would go skiing up at Hermagor, just over the border in the Austrian Alps. In spring we would go down to Krk again, enjoying empty beaches and great seascapes. In the summer, we had two great long holidays, the first to America for a month, and the second out east, to Bali, Thailand and Taiwan, where we visited friends of mine who were scientists with research jobs there.

I continued working at the university and became interested in translation, teaching classes in two or three years, while also building up my knowledge of English literature. There were composition classes which I enjoyed, imparting my knowledge of how you put an article together, a composition. Investigation and breakdown, deconstruction of articles held me in good stead, as later I would end up writing for a magazine.

In 1990, however, I fell pregnant: I use this term advisedly, as I had no intention of ever having children, although I had been attached to the coward's two girls.

Chapter Nine

A son

In accordance with my flight ethos, I more or less tried pretty hard to get rid of the baby that was growing inside me, without actually going and having a clinical abortion. A holiday had been planned with Mauro for the summer, including a long walk. We were going to walk the Pilgrims' Way in Kent, starting at Otford and ending up at Canterbury, with bed and breakfast stops each six to ten miles and company including Valerie, a good friend and Erika from Italy. It was well planned, with my parents having chipped in by going to check out the B&Bs on the route, and also having offered accommodation at their cottage in Smeeth for one of the nights during the walk. The fact of being pregnant did not deter me, but rather I decided that if the baby was strong enough to walk the Way with me, it would be well deserving to be in this world.

As it happened, it was a very warm summer. We were walking along paths in temperatures up in the high 20s. On August 5th, the day Saddam Hussein invaded Kuwait, we arrived at a B&B in Harrietsham, which had a swimming pool. Between listening to the news blaring out from the TV in the lounge, we dipped in and out of the pool on a glorious hot summer day. Indeed, I believe it was August 5th that I finally came to the conclusion that the baby may possibly be a boy.

Throughout the walk so far, we had been considering girls'

names: Selena was the obvious one, as Mauro, never loth to try a health kick, had been taking selenium. This day, instead, I started to look at boys' names. As we reached the pub we had chosen for lunch early, a young man walked in. He was an actual pilgrim: driven by a religious spirit, he had walked from London, which entailed him walking down motorways for about three days into his trip. His name was Daniel. I must have gone wittering on about names, because I promised him that if the baby was born a boy, I would name him Daniel in honour of meeting a pilgrim. However, the other name I had insisted I would be giving him was Leo, as the sun, in its scorching 30s, was in that astrological sign.

The next day we gave up. The temperature had reached 36 degrees, and we stopped at Charing, phoned my father to come and pick us up and gave up on the last three miles of a nine-mile walk from Westwell. My father later said that he was worried that the baby would be born like a roast potato! I omitted to tell him that I was tempting fate.

The experience of a long walk was positive and most enjoyable. It was not the first long walk I had done: some years previously I had walked the South Downs Way with two of the same companions. I remembered that as being quite a chore, as we had started at Eastbourne and stomped over the Seven Sisters, up and down, very tiring.

The summer passed and I returned to Italy, to the same shambles over our contracts as accompanied each academic year's beginning. However this year saw an added complication. The places were in contention for older employees who had earlier lost their jobs.

Ironically, it was Judy, who had got me the job in the first place, who was due to get her job back after an 'illegal' end to employment. Someone had to go. The head of the department at that time decided it would have to be me, because I was pregnant. In the event, I got a payout for false dismissal, but this didn't change the fact that, now pregnant, I was going to be without a job to come back to. I can't remember how much this bothered me.

The pregnancy continued and Mauro and I married. I came back to mother England to have the baby. The flight symptom was out of the window. Now the instinct was, I suppose, nesting.

The winter of 1991 saw heavy snow falls. The baby was late. Mauro and I would tramp about the woods, in twenty centimetre deep snow trying to get the labour moving. But baby wanted to stay where it was. Eventually I was taken in and induced. Labour was long. With too much information, I tried one set of aids after another: gas and air, pethidine, which more or less stopped the labour, and finally, baby boy was brought out with forceps, after thirty hours.

Any hesitation I might have had about possibly wanting to murder the child evaporated when I was lucky enough to have a stunningly beautiful baby boy, who did not look remotely like a prune. Furthermore, he latched on to my colostrum and just gazed up at me, his eyes taking in the outline of my head against the light.

The first day, abiding by the edict of not picking up baby each time he cried, I left him until I thought he should feed again, but baby Leo had the most soft and heart-rending little cry imaginable. He was soon feeding on demand, and that, unfortunately for me, meant about every hour and a half.

There was a lovely Caribbean nurse there, and I recall that we were chatting over bathing the baby. I admitted that I had never planned to have children. 'Ah' she said to me, in an accent I find impossible to write, 'the Lord knows how to help: the baby will take care of you later in life.' Meanwhile, Leo would breast feed for thirteen months and, after our return to Trieste, it would need my mother to come down and help deal with the boy in order to wean him.

Life with a darling baby boy and doting husband was mainly calm and settled. One child is easy to take around on jaunts. Leo was well-loved. Mauro doted on him and even, as a good new man, changed his nappies. We were now living in a flat with a garden. The flat was tiled throughout, with elegant tiling that I had chosen as my father had bought the flat new. There was a large *cantina,* semi-interred area, which was big enough to store my considerable library of books and where, ostensibly, I should have been writing. But there was no view in this room and I had never really got into the habit.

I had a vegetable patch: the weekends were spent either enjoying the garden or pleasurably working in it. My father and a redoubtable Serbian peasant had also created a gazebo area, which was very pleasant, with a wooden bough. I would say that for the period of a year or two, life was idyllic. Never lasts though, does it?

Mauro, meanwhile, had decided to sink all the money he had earnt into creating audiobooks for the Italian market. The project failed: no sales, no take-up. Instead Mauro had a garage full of cassettes that he had recorded and created, and which ended up being of no use to anybody. He had thrown himself into creating these audiobooks, a series of eight. Enthused by the success of these in America, he had attempted to entice an Italian market to listen to texts, read by actors.

Tom, of the broken gear story, had attempted to persuade Mauro to just create a template and then record the whole book after starting a club with subscriptions. But Mauro was adamant: he produced runs of one thousand audiobooks, pursuing his own idea, but which was never truly a success. In my opinion the Italians preferred to talk than to listen. The enterprise turned out to be a disaster. He was way before his time.

I was finally enlisted to return to work, but in a different department. There was some time before I needed to teach and instead I became pregnant again. I couldn't really believe it, and had thought I was in the menopause, but the pregnancy test was positive.

Leo would have a sibling. I was pleased about this. Both Mauro and I were only children. I don't recall what his attitude to that was, but I know that I had suffered from loneliness with my parents both out working constantly through my childhood.

I again returned to the parental home to have the baby, indeed to the same hospital. The same delay in giving birth occurred: baby didn't want to come out. It was a fifteen hour labour with finally an emergency Caesarean, but baby was born healthy and kicking at a whopping ten pounds something. Indeed, the consultant who had been following the pregnancy apologised to me and said that had he realised the baby was so big, he would have recommended an immediate Caesarean, and spared me that half a day labour.

What I recall of the birth, however, was that I was dithering about as to whether I wanted a general anaesthetic, or whether

I wanted to be awake for the operation. But by that time it was four in the morning, and I opted to be put right out. The anaesthetic only lasted a couple of hours and by six I was groggily awake and alert to the fact of Mauro holding the baby and feeding him, another little guzzler, who got through the whole bottle of baby feed. Within the day, within the morning indeed, I was able to breast feed him. Little Raphael.

The process of naming the second boy was as cerebral as the first boy. Mauro and I had looked at all sorts of names. His father had wanted us to name the boy Vittorio, but this reminded me of an oaf-like person that Mauro had brought to the house once. Also, I felt there was not a little smacking of fascist names.

We had earlier talked about calling the boy Samuel, but, again that fascist ethos prevailed in Italy when an acquaintance bluntly said we couldn't call him Samuel because it was a Jewish name. He got called Samuele as a middle name anyway. Then we liked the name Sebastian.

However, the clincher was a day trip I took with my mother and friends Pat and Maurice, down to Chiddingstone Causeway and the village of Chiddingstone, to the St. Mary the Virgin Church. Here there was a magnificent stained glass window, which portrayed the Guardian Angel Raphael and so taken was I by this image, that I resolved to call the baby Raphael. There were other resonances with this name: the shortened version Rafi, would be like the shortened version of the Swahili *rafiki* meaning friend. And wasn't there the meaning of 'respected' with the short 'raf'? This latter I never really found out and don't recall where I got the idea from anyway.

Whatever the decision, it was slightly modified by Mauro

when he went down to the Registry office, to register the birth. As he had with Leo's name. Leo came out with Leonard, which more or less sent my mother apoplectic as we thought we had agreed on Leonardo. His diminutives could have been Len, which a friend of his at school later called him, or Lennie, or even Lee, reflecting that his birth had been at Chinese New Year.

Rafi came out with a whopper of a name: Raphael Alexander Samuele Sebastiane Crampton Dazzara. That he would later be unable to read and write was an ironic twist of fate for this long naming: I would call him Raf A SS Crampton Dazzara and if there was the need to put in full names .... Well, there usually wasn't! I called him Raf or Rafi, although my mother would try and call him Raffaello! Some also tried to call him Rafe, but too similar and near to rape.

So there we were, two adults and two small children, when a shitstorm burst. I don't want to talk about it, but suffice it to say that with Rafi just three months old, I had another psychotic episode. What I remember is repeated dreams that I was dead, or even that I was a coloured toy brick in the garden, flummoxed as to how I would get back to being a human being, locked in. Mauro is intrigued by this expression of an altered state of consciousness, but the truth was that at the time I was too afraid to talk to him about it.

Baby would need to be weaned, as my drug regime would have fed through into him. I kept producing milk and had to be milked like a cow, to get rid of the surplus. My father-in-law was perturbed and accused his son of being an idiot for getting involved with a woman who had mental problems. I don't really think there was much love lost between me and my in-laws.

72

In the interim, my parents returned to Trieste to help out with their mad daughter and the two babies. It was through the summer, it was hot. Eventually my mother persuaded the doctors that I should be taken in to an institution. However, in Italy, these institutions were open, and clients were allowed to come and go. One afternoon, I was taken to the nearest accommodation. In my mind I could not just walk out (although I could have done), but eager to get out of the place, I tied together a couple of sheets that had been left in the bathroom in lieu of towels and climbed out of the window.

The sheets untied and I ended up crashed on the ground with two broken feet and two compression fractures in the back, spent a few days in hospital and then was sent home to convalesce. Eventually I was given a brace to wear for the next six months, to keep my back straight. By Christmas I was near taking it off, and recall having had a small accident at a crossroads as I was driving and becoming most agitated that the insurance would know I was wearing a brace and decline the insurance claim. That didn't happen.

We spent Christmas in England with my family. By this time Rafi was nine months old and not sitting up at all. Over the following months my father-in-law would insist there was something wrong with him. In the event he was right.

That summer, I took Rafi to a local paediatrician who asked a number of questions and looked at the boy, who was now handsome and sturdy, but still, over a year old, wearing nappies. He was almost non-verbal, but would make little noises to communicate and if he wanted something, he would grab my hand and pull it to show what it was. The paediatrician suggested that if I were going back to England, we should try to see a specialist there. He agreed with my father-in-law that there was some sort of cognitive delay: the boy should be able to take instructions and go into another room to fetch (like a dog). For Mauro it was hard, I think he found it difficult to relate to a baby who was not communicative in a properly functioning manner.

I found life highly constraining: the situation of having to take care of two small children was just so different from the world of work that I had experienced for the previous two decades, that I felt I was getting cabin fever. Mauro had decided that instead of taking Leo into the kindergarten (which he hated and cried tempestuously about each morning), he was going to go swimming. So I was left to get the boys up and dressed and get the older child to kindergarten by 8 or 8.30 in the morning, or whatever it was.

Certainly having children in your forties makes more inroads into stamina than being a young mother. By mid-morning I was exhausted. Mauro by now had ended up with an office and a sales team selling large format art books and encyclopaedias, which was a tough business. He would be out till nine each night. Inevitably I cooked his dinner and left it for him, but would crash out at about the time I got the boys to bed. The idyll was a bit stale. Often Mauro would go in to work on a Saturday, and of course there was the tangential problem that he, out all week, liked to spend the weekend at home, while I, stuck in the house during that time, couldn't wait till the weekend to get out and about. I think I made some cursory attempt to get back to work, but it was half hearted and if the truth were known, I hated teaching English.

From the psychotic episode I was still on medication but

in the autumn of 1995 I said I couldn't stand it any more and fled back to England with both the boys and the promise to Mauro that I would try and get well.

Chapter Ten

Upheaval

It is a moot point how useful it is to flee a situation. I had fled back to England a previous time, at my father's behest, when I went into a depression in Trieste. But I am not sure the lesson that it can do no good was actually learnt. Here I was fleeing a situation I found difficult to tolerate once again. I was not really prepared for a life with two small children and no possibility of adult company for the whole working week. Back in the UK, there was adult company, but my parents were getting old.

We slipped into a routine. Without consciously choosing and deciding that we would live in England, I found a nursery for Leo and we began to deal with the problem that was Rafi. In addition I attempted to address my own problem.

I went to see the GP and was referred to a psychiatrist. He immediately said that the problem was the Italian health authorities were giving me the wrong medicine: I was on Modecate, a medicine that could cause depression, rather than the Depixol which would treat it. Changing the medication should alleviate the terrible blanket of sloth and low mood that bedevilled me.

With respect to Rafi, the GP referred him to the consultant paediatrician and he was enrolled in the Children's Centre, a specialist unit for children with developmental problems. At two he was still not talking. Thus began a process of diagnosing Rafi's problems. The consultant paediatrician said quite adamantly 'he is not autistic, he is definitely not autistic'. I recall she looked at me as if she thought this might be news, but in fact I had never considered that Rafi could be autistic, not that I knew much about autism then. However, after a couple of regular check-ups, the same paediatrician said 'he is autistic, he is definitely autistic.'

By this time I had been looking into the condition and knew that there was a possible test, a blood test. When I mentioned this to the paediatrician at the next check-up, she said, 'Oh, haven't I prescribed that?' Amazingly, to take blood, a young male nurse was despatched to our home, and very competently distracted Rafi while he took the requisite blood sample. We waited for the result. It came back that Rafi was positive for the condition Fragile X syndrome, the second largest cause of developmental delay in boys. He would be dependent for his entire life, but most probably would not have physical disabilities. I don't know if there was any relief when the paediatrician told me he would live a healthy life into his seventies. What I do recall is that my father would frequently admit to spending sleepless nights worrying about what would happen to Rafi. Mauro seemed to take it in his stride, up to a point, although when the two boys were small, he didn't pay much attention to Rafi. He, I think, found it difficult to relate to a boy who wouldn't or couldn't talk. The rate of divorce amongst couples with autistic children is high.

Rafi's diagnosis of Fragile X syndrome led to the rest of the family being tested. It turned out that my mother was a carrier, although how that happened I don't know because I had been given to think that the chromosome problem passed from fathers. I too was a carrier, and Leo had an above average number of CagT protein repeats, which is a symptom of the condition. This, although we did not know it at the time, was to be a burden for Leo, as scientists were beginning to discover that male carriers of the gene were developing Ataxia in middle age, that is a sort of Parkinson's disease, with tremor. Rafi's story is, however, the subject of a whole new volume.

Meanwhile I started frequenting mothers and toddlers groups and indeed, I ended up going to three. This permitted me to make friends, there were other mothers who were older and had small children. It was a lifeline, something that in Italy is performed by the sisters, mothers and aunts of babies.

A very important lifeline was held out to me in the form of an invitation to join a writing group. A woman who became a firm friend suggested I join her creative writing group at the local Adult Education centre. It was spring. The group was actually nearing the end, for the summer, but come autumn I joined. I was lucky. I had my mother and father to take care of the children while I went out for a couple of hours once a week. Mauro, meanwhile, kept in constant contact, but one day, when he was in Sandgate, and I was driving along, he said to me, quite flatly 'you're not coming back are you?' This put me on the spot. I had not really considered what I was doing, mainly just trying to keep my head above water, but he was right: I had enough support systems here to feel less burdened and was unlikely to go back to the lovely flat and garden in Trieste.

Eventually Mauro would take a lover and this consolidated the decision, that I should divorce. It was tough on Leo. He was extremely attached to his father. He even said he would throw himself off the White Cliffs of Dover if we divorced. And Rafi? Well the question of losing a relation would come up for him a couple of decades later, when he too went into a depression.

Despite our divorce, however, Mauro stayed very regularly in contact and visits from him to UK, and for us to go to Trieste proceeded apace. My parents were doting grandparents and an absolute rock for my floundering self. The situation with Rafi was still one with some difficulty, but I managed to find a support group, which was held under the aegis of the National Autistic Society and while it turned out that Rafi's health situation was complicated, the support group allowed us to meet people and while away the time.

So gradually a network of friends grew up around me, and in addition this permitted me to develop some interests. The writing was definitely one of the most important lifelines, and it is one I would like to give other people who find themselves in difficulties. Coupled with the writing came an interest in discussing, with a couple of the mothers I had met, most amazingly a woman from Leeds and who I had known then, who had in the interim years spent time in Greece and Zimbabwe, and then ended up in Hythe.

The writing also led on to other things, eventually to remunerated employment. This was the result of another serendipitous meeting. I was a jazz fan and read in the local papers that saxophonist John Surman was playing at St. Mary's Church in Ashford. I went along to listen. The local paper also said 'local resident', so I looked in the telephone directory and found his name. I had the temerity to phone. John Surman was distinctly cordial and not fazed by my fan enthusiasm.

He agreed to meet and we met in a pub not far from home. He brought me a copy of one of his latest discs. He was kind enough to ask about me, and I started wittering on about the writers' group. Promptly he said I could interview him. This put me on the spot.

However, I had seen in the doctor's surgery copies of the magazine *Kent Life*. So I phoned up the editor and asked whether *prima facie* they might be interested in an interview. It all came about, not only my text and interview but my photographic portrait of John, on a blustery late spring day down on Romney Marsh. Eventually I wound up writing a lot of articles for the magazine and that was a link that would continue to this day, with some changes along the way, as I ended up writing about artists, monthly. This did not happen until my father fell mortally ill, however.

My father took the place of Leo's own father. This is something Leo has admitted to me in his adult years. My father was a rock. He supported me and indeed it was his idea that I should get a computer to write with. I would take the children to school and then come back and sit and write in my room. I churned out short stories for the creative writing class, and then stories for a writing group which grew out of the classes when those stopped. Eventually I would write up my articles on my computer and when the technology appeared, I would be able to email copy. I also wrote reams of accounts of how the children were progressing which I sent off to Mauro.

Leo went from the nursery to a Catholic primary school. At the time I had been swayed by a friend in education into thinking that the Catholic schools offered the best education. In the end, I feel that Leo was disadvantaged by the fact that he was not a practising Catholic. Indeed when it got to year 6, I even investigated changing schools for him, as I never felt that his skills, which he hid under a bushel, were being adequately developed.

In the end, I decided that it would be too much upheaval for him to change schools just before the Kent Test. He had made some good friends at the school, but none who stayed with him till his adult years. He took the Kent Test, Kent's version of the 11-plus, but barely scraped through in mathematics. They had had something like four teachers in their last year for the teaching of maths, and that was a severe disadvantage.

From primary Leo went on to the local grammar school. I will never forget the day I went to pick him up from school. I have never seen, before or since, my loving son look so desperately sad. He had cried, it is true, on his last day at his primary school, but this day he looked totally bowed under and despondent. I ate my heart out wondering if I had done the right thing, for we had appealed the decision on the Kent Test, to get him a place at the grammar. His friends and the other cohort from the primary, were going down the road to Dover to the Catholic school there. I had rebelled against this, as the OFSTED results there had been poor both in maths, where Leo was already disadvantaged, but also in art, which was, *par excellence*, Leo's forte. Years later Leo would come out with stories of the boys' misbehaviour, which was not far off the public school antics of the boys in Lindsay Anderson's *If.* Within about a year of Leo going to grammar, my father would pass away, leaving Leo without a strong male model in his existence.

Life with Rafi was not a bed of roses. Getting him into the

right educational establishments was a fight all along. From the Children's Centre, he obtained a place at Hythe Infants Special language unit, but he could not keep up with the academic levels of the children there and we were soon looking at a place in the local special school. He was at school there till he was 16, but he never really learnt to read properly, although he could point out the TV programmes he wanted to watch in the *Radio Times* when we had it, or in the paper. When he was about nine, he had an epileptic seizure. I managed to take him to the doctor's surgery from where he was taken to hospital. He would not be medicated unless he had a second attack. Which he did. And then a third, when he landed up in hospital again, having had a fit at school which did not diminish when we administered rectal Valium for him. From then on he was medicated.

Although he had no further seizures, he began to have panic attacks, fairly regularly, almost monthly. He would go very white, heart beating fast and he would get shaky. Sometimes he would vomit. Other times, it was as if he was having an attack of Tourette's: he would swear. Most often he would crave comfort, a big hug would help him out of his attack. Repeated accounts of this behaviour were given to the doctor and the paediatrician, as I thought this was perhaps *petit mal*, a form of epilepsy, but the only thing the doctors came back with was panic and anxiety.

So through most of the boys' school years, I was at home, with my parents, years that passed in a flash.

Chapter Eleven

Home?

I was medicated throughout all these years. (I still am.) I would have a monthly injection, which meant that for two days or so I was semi-comatose, and then emerged into a sense of normality until the next injection. I hated this up/down routine, and so gradually stretched out the periods between getting the nurse to inject me. This was no good at all and eventually I spiralled into another bout of psychosis, entailing a couple of weeks in the local hospital's psychiatric ward and leaving my parents to fend for my children. I remember being afraid that the boys would be taken into care, but the psychiatric nurse delegated to me, reassured me that this was unlikely to happen. Nor did she think I would get ECT, electro-convulsive therapy which frightened me. There was no change in the medication that I recall, but I was under observation, eventually to be let out.

Mauro would telephone me almost daily in the relatively public lounge area of the psychiatric ward (which is no longer there, note). There were regular three- or six-monthly appointments with the consultant psychiatrist. She eventually got as near to a cure for me as it was possible to be. She had noticed that I was having involuntary mouth twitches and she decided to change my medication. From the Depixol, I was to take Risperdal. This was a distinct improvement for me on the injections and I felt far more like my old (unmedicated) self. The major side effect, however, was weight gain. So, fat and happy, or slim and beleaguered? Those were the options. I had had enough of depression and psychosis and was just glad that I felt much better, with my mental capacities feeling sharper again.

One of the regular events in my life had been meeting for dinner with a small group, just four of us, of women who had strong interests in philosophy and religion. Each dinner event was also the site of deep inquiry into the nature of the world and ways of looking at it. Two of the women were Christians, one a Buddhist and myself, well, just an agnostic really. I sat on the rim of the discussions. What did I bring away from them? An appreciation of compassion and tolerance.

One of the women told me about an art history course which Tate Modern was holding online. This became the start of a long, enjoyable and fruitful journey for me, ultimately ending in a total career shift. I signed up for the course, which took place over a year. It was free. However a second level was also offered, which had to be paid for. I took this course too.

Having dipped into academia again, I wondered what I could do next and looked into Open University courses. Over the next couple of years I undertook a couple of Art History units at the OU. These included studying from home, writing essays and also a written exam at the end of the session. The study materials included CDs to watch at home, and a series of very fine text books. I revelled in this study, finding it a perfect blend of social history and creativity. Having finished two, or maybe three units, I then looked into continuing studying at the University of Kent and found that the OU units would be added as credits. This was before university fees were hiked to such awful heights, so I signed up for a BA in History and Philosophy of Art. Of course I was lucky because I had the use of a car and could drive over to Canterbury two or three times a week to undertake the course. Eventually I graduated in 2013.

My father died in 2003. His demise was fairly sudden. He was suffering and couldn't seem to eat. Furthermore he had difficulty sleeping from discomfort. He was taken into hospital and died two weeks later. Rafi did not come to the funeral. But when we went up to the cemetery to pay our respects with my mother, there was one moment when Rafi tried to look under the planks which had been placed over my father's grave. Whether he was trying to see if my father, his Nonno, was there or not, one can only guess.

While he was alive, my father had invested in a house for me and the boys. We lived there just a short while, because when my father died, my mother found she was too frightened to be in her house alone at night. Hence I, with Leo and Rafi, moved back in with her. I remember at the time it felt like a burden, but the truth was that she would sit with Rafi, permitting me a considerable amount of freedom. She was, generally, able-bodied. We had a home help, Sandra, who was a treasure and used to take her out in the mornings in her car to do odd bits of shopping. Mainly I would prepare an evening meal for us all, and Mum would have had cold meats and a slice of bread for her lunch.

At the weekend we often went out to eat. In the summer I would organise somebody to stay in the house with her, while I and the boys went to Italy to visit their father. One carer was quite obstreperous and when I got back complained that my mother would start drinking at three in the afternoon. Mum never drank much, but one could argue that a campari soda was a strong affair.

Thence continued a life with my mother again. I have a lot of regrets about this, despite the fact that friends said I did well. I don't think I was particularly kind to my mother. Most of the time, if the weather was good, I would sit out on the terrace reading. Mum used to watch the TV and follow the games Rafi would play. She would frequently complain that she was 'left alone like a dog', expecting us to sit with her and entertain her. Years later I find in a drawer a note saying 'YOU LIVE HERE WITH DIANA AND THE BOYS. YOU HAVE NOTHING TO WORRY ABOUT, LEO IS NOT ILL.' The wonderful Sandra, who by now was almost as much a carer as I, had evidently responded to some anxiety of my mother's.

The day Rafi had the epileptic seizure he got taken to hospital. When he had another two, as mentioned above, he was put on medication.

Meanwhile, with my mother at home and Rafi at a special school, out all day, I plodded on with my art history studies. I enjoyed the reading, but as usual I was hindered by my failure to read very fast. And reading slowly was not compensated for by remembering everything, so my studies were quite laborious.

One day my mother got out of bed and fell. It was seven in the morning. I looked at her and immediately phoned the ambulance, for I thought she might have had a stroke. Leo was still living at home then, and old enough to drive, and the car would come and pick Rafi up for school, so I was able to delegate Leo and speed up to the hospital to check on Mum, who I found in A&E. We sat around for a while and some tests were done. Mum had banged her thorax on the side cabinet and a big bruise developed, but apparently no ribs were broken. Nor did they think she had had a stroke. She was sent home.

Unfortunately the shock of falling had made her afraid to walk. She didn't seem to be able to put one foot in front of the other anymore and teetered. I got the nursing agency to come in and take care of her through the night. But I was unable to sleep and thus had two very bad nights. I immediately called up a care home to see if they could take her. They agreed. Leo at this stage was away in Amsterdam with his college. Mum was taken into the care home and stayed there a week.

When Leo came back, we went in to see her, and found that she was almost comatose. An ambulance was called and she was taken into hospital, where the diagnosis was simply dehydration. They obviously weren't taking that much care of her. There had anyway been some concern as to whether they could take her with dementia. She had been diagnosed with vascular dementia a couple of years earlier, but was still well enough at that stage for me to take care of her at home, despite some angry outbursts, which I am told were characteristic for dementia sufferers.

My experience of looking at homes to find somewhere for her was awful. The minute you mentioned dementia, you were shown onto wards where the smell of urine predominated. The care home she had been in and who had not given her enough water had decided that she couldn't go back there. By sheer chance, really, I popped into another care home, which was situated in a quiet residential area and found the owner, who agreed to visit the hospital to assess my mother. Fortunately he felt totally able to care for her with his staff, and she was transferred out of the hospital, after about a week, into this care home.

I was confident that she was receiving good care there and she was there for about two years. Unfortunately she was on the path to a steady decline and got very thin and frail. I would visit every day for a short while. Gradually she seemed to lose the capacity to speak. Frequently, though, she would say something about Diana, and I would point to myself and say 'who am I? I am Diana'. She would give a sweet little smile, and a nod as if to say how silly. There's a book to write about dementia, because Mum veered from this sweet little old lady, to an angry harridan, as anyone who has dealt with a dementia patient can empathise with. For me, this slow decline was a sort of heartbreak and I still feel overwhelmed with emotion thinking about her.

I went away in the early autumn of 2011. Mum was taken into hospital again. She was bedevilled by urinary tract infections, which would come on and make her a bit doolally until they found the correct antibiotic. From Italy I asked if I should cut my holiday short, but the staff said no, she would be okay. When I got back, she was very weak. Within a month, she eventually faded forever. It was November.

For some reason my mother had confided in my father that she thought I hated her. This is the barometer of how my levels of kindness must have failed. Losing her was awful. My heart still wells at memories of her, years on. She had been a wonderful mother, tenacious, persevering, generous, humorous. A delight and a clever, though unfulfilled woman. She had doted on Leo, with whom she had a very close and loving relationship and she had been stalwart when dealing with the frequently very difficult Rafi. She was usually equable with me, but in the latter days there might be frequent bouts of shouting, as the dementia took hold. This notwithstanding, my memories of my mother are sweet.

Chapter Twelve

Pendulum

Travel, which had been such a big part of my early life, with years in Ethiopia and Kenya and a couple of fantastic tourist trips to the US and to East Asia with Mauro, was more restricted with two children. We ended up leading a sort of pendulum life, swinging backwards and forwards from Trieste. Ultimately this meant that my elder son grew up with the same sort of yearning to live in Italy which had coloured my own adolescence and early years. Why I didn't go to live in Italy when I was 22, just graduated, and therefore available for a future as an English teacher was a moot point. I was after more exciting things, and succeeded in getting the job in Ethiopia.

The experiences I had in Ethiopia were distinctly character-forming. In addition, I was living on an agricultural development unit and came into contact with experts and workers in development. This was what prepared me for the postgraduate course in Development Studies in Bath. Whilst I was in Ethiopia the revolution took place. When I studied politics in my course, I read about military coups, and noted that the Ethiopian case was textbook. A liberal wing of the military attempts to replace a dictator. Hardened rightwingers within the army stage a *putsch* to displace the military and, as Napoleon said, once the revolutionaries get into power, their first job is to replace the revolutionaries. My boyfriend of the time said I had to leave: his was the impetus to try and do the course in Bath, and I packed and left. He was right, as I have described above. It was a frightening time.

I have already told the tale of how the Bath Diploma became Ph.D research, and that led me back to East Africa for the year to study the tourism industry and language. In effect, I had a very negative view of tourism. There was a sort of snobbery in this; I didn't consider myself a tourist, I was a *traveller* - although see more on this below. Indeed my history was one of travel, in childhood to Italy, which would become a second home, then at university the first time, a year in France, where I travelled around, then those important years in Ethiopia and a year in Kenya. Because I was a traveller, I felt that I had a better grip on understanding other cultures: I was certainly reading about them. Tourism, instead, was a ticket to forming and reinforcing stereotypes, gained first in the home country. My research took into account the images posted in tourism publicity. These conformed strictly to an ideology of difference, seen in structuralist terms with antonymous dichotomies: black/white, nature/ culture, female/male, rural/ urban, traditional/ modern, where the first of the couplet is the so-called unmarked category, the one who holds and wields power, so the obverse of what I have written above: white/black, culture/nature, male/female, urban/rural, modern/traditional. So why do we need to diss the 'other' in order to establish our own identity?

Once I had finished my Ph.D I was ready to look for work in Italy. Whilst there I was able to travel down to Croatia, also going as far as Belgrade and Zagreb before the breakup of Yugoslavia.

I taught English at the University and eventually got pregnant: the two things not linked! Mauro was a sweet and accommodating husband, but being with two small children was utterly overwhelming for me. Despite this, there was some travel with the family, pure tourism. One holiday was spent in the Balearic islands when Leo was just about a year old. That was a real beach holiday, with days spent pottering down to the sea, or swimming at the pool.

Travelling with two children was more complicated and more expensive. I remember on one occasion, I travelled back to England alone with Leo about four and Rafi in a pushchair. A woman in the queue said to me 'well done' as I manoeuvred children and cases at the arrivals lounge. This was about the time I was going to stay.

As I became established in the UK, going backwards and forwards to Italy became our summer norm. This was however punctuated by a holiday in Portugal, where a good friend, Ahmed (whose cousin put me up in Kenya, as mentioned above) was having a large party for about a hundred guests. A hotel with a pool was organised for us to stay in. Many of the guests used this facility and we got to know several interesting people. The boys were at that stage fourteen and sixteen years old, and Leo was adequately happy to accompany us. Pure tourism again. I recall I had a stinking cold and didn't use the pool, which I normally love.

This small snapshot is enough to show that even when apparently settled in one country, over the years we had covered quite a few miles, and had a fairly large carbon footprint, as we travelled by plane.

Travel has changed a lot in forty years. The number of people flying is huge. Even at the time I was writing my thesis in the late 1970s, tourism was billed as the largest industry in the world, after the arms industry. Nonetheless a further huge percentage of the world's population had never flown in a plane.

What has intrigued me about all this movement has been the way people are classified. Movement from the so-called First World to the so-called Third World is tourism or development. There is the joke about the difference between an expert and a specialist expert: the former has flown over the country in the dark, the latter has flown over the country in the day, in the nonetheless huge business of development.

Movement from the so-called Third World or the periphery is mainly classed as immigration, with migration being the result of war, poverty, drought and famine. Immigration means people may attempt to settle. Migration covers the huge populace of the dispossessed, who have little chance of settling and, at worst, may be shuttled backwards between centre and periphery mercilessly. War in the Middle East has meant that hapless millions, as at the time of the Second World War, are now moving, frequently on foot and across seas in perilous boats. Emblazoned in my mind are images of Rwandans fleeing murder, as well as streams of migrants trying to cross into Europe before the barbed wire is strung across borders. Another word for a traveller: refugee.

The demonisation of travel may be reflected in the term traveller itself, which has overtaken the term gypsy, considered derogatory. On a Europe-wide canvas, the traveller community is relegated to Roma, a group of people who apparently originated in northern India and spread westwards.

There are also millions of young people and students now

going on what are called gap years, notably between school and university in Europe and Australia. This has become such an institution that companies exist which organise the travel: a contemporary take on the package tours which blossomed with the era of cheaper air travel (for Europeans) in the 1960s. This is a symptom of freedom and wealth. For me it is also a moot point as to whether this had the magical ability to open people's minds, as was hoped in the grand period of package tours.

I have talked myself into a corner, where both the freedom to travel and the possession of something called a home are privileges, implying a certain level of wealth. (In the two years I have been writing this, the number of refugees has gone up to 70 million.) But now consider this! With the fiftieth anniversary of the moon landings, a radio programme tells us about trips into space. Some billionaires are considering spending 200,000 dollars, or was it pounds, for a trip into space. We have already seen the attempt by Richard Branson to get a flight out of the earth's atmosphere, an attempt which failed. However, some have already signed up for this new jaunt, which is scheduled, *ceteris paribus*, to take place in 2023. That's just short years away. There has even been talk of a hotel area in the space station. This is no longer travel to go and find or explore another culture, but rather cocking a snook at the familiar and the terrestrial in search of greater kicks. For thousands of pounds. I suppose many thoughts of the intrinsic curiosity of the human animal come to mind. If it's there, go and do it. At the back of people's minds it is possible to see that proposed lunar colonies might resolve the problem of an increasingly overcrowded earth. Or is it the competitiveness of 'me first', getting to do what few others do? How does a person who is going into space consider the dangers of space travel? Is it a concealed impetus for suicide in a dramatic fashion? However, this is certainly a twenty-first century consideration and concern. Rather them than me.

This is history now. The pandemic of Covid 19 has locked down millions in their houses, flats, shanties, big or small, comfortable or hovels. It has grounded airlines and is changing the world in dramatic ways.

Chapter Thirteen

Family again

I admitted to a friend I was writing a memoir. 'Well,' she said, 'you have had an interesting life and have travelled', which I hope I have brought alive in what I've written. 'You might write about your mother,' she said. 'She was a strong woman.' She was right of course. My mother was made of stern stuff and was like a beacon in a storm for me, always there. So, in cyclical fashion, I began with the family and I return to my family.

My mother had met my father when he was out in Italy, just after the war. She was the interpreter for the town major in the Allied Military Government of the Free Territory of Trieste (AMGFTT), having studied English. She had been enrolled into the famous *Ca' Foscari*, the Venetian university, but had her studies curtailed due to the war and the danger of travelling back and forth to Venice. Her own mother suffered poor health, with a weak heart, which is what finally caused her demise. She also had two brothers, but one of these died of meningitis when very young, leaving her with an adored brother, eleven years her younger. She had admitted to me that she had a nervous breakdown at the beginning of the war, but not much was ever said of this.

Whilst out riding her bicycle in the countryside one day, going to work for the major, she had been strafed by a British plane and had thrown herself into a ditch to survive. My father would joke that he had liberated her, and that he had decided to marry her and bring her back to England to avoid her being tarred and feathered. Both these events were recounted in an almost throw-away fashion. My father would laugh. They married within two months of meeting, a whirlwind romance.

My mother had, early on, a hard time integrating into British life. In particular, when her mother died, she lost a lot of weight and was grieving, a factor which a counsellor I had gone to had said would have percolated down into my own psyche, occurring as it did when I was about seven years old and possibly predisposing me to depression in later life. I recall her in my childhood earning a few pence mending stockings, as I mentioned, in an era when these were not throw-away. She was also usually very willing to spend time playing with me.

My mother was a slave to housework. This may account for why I am such a slob, because she put me off. Always with my head in a book, rather than wielding a hoover (or a Dyson). Later on she would open a little clothes shop in the 'village' we lived in and she had the shop long enough for me both to benefit from having lovely clothes and for me to work there on Saturdays. Remarkably I recall her having sent me off to Central London to her suppliers to select clothes for the shop. Shubette dresses, I remember it well. I used to go to Central London with her and help choose, so she must have trusted me.

It was all relatively comfortable, bar those quarterly rows, which seemed to be most often related to periods of increased drinking and drunkenness in my father.

The story goes that when he was courting her, back in the days in Friuli, he was already drinking a lot. My mother tried to end the relationship with him, on account of his drunkenness, but she mentioned to me that he would beg her and promise not to drink anymore. In my teens, there was a notorious event when they went out to the local club and Dad was so drunk he got into a fight. Mum walked out, thinking that he would see this and follow her, but he apparently just calmed down and started to offer everybody drinks. More money than sense.

Mum got home and poured all the alcoholic drinks in the cabinet down the sink. When Dad got a lift home, goodness knows what time of the morning, Mum put him in the car, and drove him back to my grandpa's house and tried to get him to stay there. Poor Pop, my grandpa: I don't think he knew what a soak he had as a son. Dad hardly knew what he had been doing, but was told about it the next day by the mother of my boyfriend, who was also there, and he stopped drinking completely for a (short) while, retreating into the garage where he had a worktable, and would do some carpentry work. The sobriety would never really last that long.

Right into the era when Leo was small, my father would drink vast amounts of gin. Frankly I don't know how he managed to focus. At work he seemed to start drinking at lunchtime. In my teens he would most frequently come home already drunk, and there would be an air of tension around the dinner table that was almost unbearable. I used to say my parents were still fighting the Second World War between them.

When I went away to university at the age of 18, my mother told me that for a while my father was kinder. She had felt bereft, having only one child – they never managed to have other children, despite trying – but nothing to the proto-be-reavement she would feel when, after university, I went off to

Ethiopia. According to my grandfather, who, at that time had moved in with Mum and Dad, she would cry regularly. How close this mother-daughter relationship.

I think my parents were pleased when I finally got a job in Trieste and seemed to settle down. However, my mental state was not totally stable. There was another breakdown. My mother came down to take care of me. I remember her clearly, she was so worried. I didn't seem to be able to get out of the severe depression I was in. Total melancholy. The coward had ditched me, and she thought that the conditions under which he did this were reprehensible. They were, of course. How can you leave someone when they are in need of you? Depression, however, is a relationship breaker.

This was the point, as mentioned, that my father suggested I go back to England for a spell to get better. It wasn't a solution. It was at this point I tried consciously to take my own life, leading to a period in hospital, until I got better. I did get better. I am not sure how. I have said this before, I am not clear how one gets better. My ex-husband, after yet another period of poor mental health when I had the two children, reported that my psychiatrist of that time, a very nice and empathetic man, had nonetheless told him that psychosis could last a day, a week, or go on forever. He tells me this now with some humour, but it does point to the fact that mental states are hard to identify and psychiatry is almost an inexact science. It also suggests that my current state of relative contentment is paradisiacal.

With that later period of mental instability, I upped roots and came back to England again, as noted, this time with my two children. Fortunately for me my parents had space to accommodate us.

This was supposed to be about my mother. Her stalwartness must have saved me. However anxious and worried she may have been, she always put on a brave front. When Leo was born, I think she was over the moon, as was my father. My mother, in particular, developed a very close and loving relationship with Leo. One day she choked back tears and said she felt she had never been loved the way Leo loved her.

My father doted on the boys too, but was particularly attached to Rafi, as he had been the one to oversee Rafi's weaning, when I had to take medication and could no longer breastfeed the child who was by then three months old. Dad would also be very positive when we tried Rafi on a gluten-free diet, meaning Rafi always had different meals when he was small and Dad would put a gloss on this, telling him his food was 'special'.

By this time Dad was drinking non-alcoholic beer and had abandoned his diet of gin-martinis. I am not sure what cured him of that. Perhaps just the vision of his two small grandchildren, with a father who was not really that paternal. Indeed Leo would later comment that his maternal grandfather was practically the male father-figure for him.

I am not sure I have given a picture of my father bar his drinking. He was, however, someone with a wicked sense of humour for which he was appreciated by his friends, by Mauro and by myself of course. When sober, he was just that, sober and calm, so difficult to perceive these amazing contradictions and the fire in his character when drunk. He had some thirty employees in his Renault dealership business and he felt that he was their father too, as he said they would come to him for advice. The mind boggles! I think his younger partners were also partly scared by him, for he could be blatantly rude and I think he didn't tolerate fools. I remember him wrily saying 'nobody likes me,' but in fact they did. His friends sought out his company and he had strong sentiments of loyalty to his friends, which must have been appreciated.

My father died rather quickly. He had been suffering and had been to the doctor, who was ineffectual. It wasn't till I went in with Dad and noticed how self-effacing he was with the doctor, that I realised he had not really been admitting how poorly he felt, not sleeping and not eating. When I impressed upon the doctor his poor state of health, he was told to go and have a series of blood tests, but this was too little too late. Within three weeks he was dead, after a period of two weeks in hospital.

My mother carried on for another eight years, somewhat to my surprise, as I had rather thought of her as being the weaker in health of the two. However, she sank into vascular dementia and life with her was frequently, perhaps even constantly, a worry. I was helped along the way by a home help who was really much more than that, someone who became part of the family and helped out almost beyond the bounds of duty. Surprisingly, when Mum was tested for dementia, her mathematics were still good.

When my mother developed dementia, she would sometimes get very angry. There was a dementia helpline in Canterbury and on at least three occasions I phoned up and bemoaned the state of my poor mother. The lady on the end of the line made it quite clear to me that dementia is a cruel illness. My mother could not help herself from her bouts of anger. I recall my mother's refrain: 'you leave me alone like a dog.' This was pretty strong, considering I was in the house with her all afternoon and sleeping there in her house, rather than in my own abode. The children were there with her. She was hardly alone. The truth of the matter was, though - as I've already admitted - that if the weather was good, through the clement months of April to October, I would be out on the terrace with my head in a book.

She had said I would regret putting her in a home, but the situation with Rafi was difficult. He did not understand her weakness and was abrupt and rude with her. The home took good care of her, but it broke my heart as she said she 'wanted to get back to where I live.' Over time her speech went. She would whisper incomprehensibly. One day she mentioned her mother, who, she said, was in the room next door. She really just faded away, getting thinner and thinner and looking sadder and sadder. Even her death certificate said that the death was caused by immobility. There is no easy way out.

Chapter Fourteen

Conclusion

I am coming up to the eighth decade of my existence, feeling enormously happy that I am still alive. More importantly, I have had twenty years without another episode of psychosis, bar one very funny turn, which passed quickly. Is it worth talking about? Perhaps not. Suffice it to say that it concerned my lack of trust in getting involved with a man, and that I was right in that, as he turned out to be a philanderer, but basically strongly tied to the wife who abandoned him.

Significantly, I have a band of friends who know about my mental illness, but are not fazed by it, and an ex-husband who remains in contact and is still supportive. These things are definitely important.

What would I say to someone who is suffering from mental illness? Please find someone to talk to. A hard deal in these times of austerity and restricted (even non-existent) mental health services. I note that my local hospital no longer has the psychiatric unit and wonder what happens to the mentally ill, albeit there is frequent news of the paucity of help for sufferers, and news of finances being poured into services for the ill. It seems to me obtuse that there is more in the media on mental health problems, while services are getting fewer and more difficult to access.

For my own part, I have vowed never to get ill again and am

cognisant of the sorts of situations which could tip me over: not eating and not sleeping, a couple of basic elements. Getting into deep emotional waters: to steer clear of.

Professional advice increasingly demands private payment. On the other hand, looking back, those groups that I found have been invaluable: the women who ate and talked; even the Tate online group, whose forays into art took me out of myself; a monthly reading group, also taking me out of myself; a writing group where I could build the narrative of my existence, but where, writing fictional short stories, I could indulge creativity.

I met the psychiatrist who I believe helped me heal. I asked her if I could stop taking the medication (fat and happy), but she said that even after a long period of good health, it was possible that I could relapse. I didn't want to risk that at all and continue to take a low dose of respiridone, which seems to balance me. The proof of the pudding.....

I worried that bereavement, losing my mother and my father, would tip me over into psychosis. I was actually present at the deaths of both my mother and my father and, perhaps oddly, it felt like a privilege to accompany them beyond. Bereavement didn't tip me into psychosis. This does not mean that I didn't grieve. I still do now, years on, with a sometimes overwhelming feeling of pity, regret and sadness for my mother who was so stalwart, and Dad, the rock, who was so conflicted.

My children have taken me well beyond myself, with the preoccupation that they could inherit my psychotic disposition, but concerning myself with trying to keep them free of situations which would make them ill. It is difficult to inure others to life's knocks, however.

Rafi grew up fit and healthy, but the marriage of his older

brother seemed to knock him for six. Rafi stopped eating, almost became bulimic, frequently retching when food was presented to him. I would say now that he has a borderline eating disorder, Prader-Willi syndrome, eating till he is almost sick. At the time I got him referred to a psychiatrist experienced with special needs people. Rafi had more or less also stopped talking.

On the other hand, he spoke to me about getting organised for his wedding. He needed a menu and a red carpet. It broke my heart to tell him that he would need to find someone who would marry him. He had a crush on a young actress we had met. This goes on. He may well sit and look really sad, and when I ask him what is wrong, he points to the T-shirt he has of her and her fellow actresses, and sobs.

Rafi got very thin through that period of Leo's wedding. He actually managed to retch when we sat down for the wedding lunch, which meant I had to haul him off to the room we were staying in, and got some food brought up for us there. We couldn't have him vomiting over his sister-in-law's festivities, especially since she is a vomitophobe (so was I, but it is amazing what you get used to).

The psychiatrist was on the verge of medicating him for a depression. However, he noted that 30 per cent of people have no response to anti-depressants, which work only on some 30 per cent of the populace. At that time we did not medicate him, and over a period of about six months, Rafi gradually started to eat again, and also started to talk more. He had frequent panic attacks, and over the last four years or so, these have started to be less frequent, although the regularity of them, about monthly, made me think there may be something cyclical in them.

The social services had their input into his lack of talking. They created for him a communication passport with a couple of little books which had pictures in of, for example, food he might like to eat, plus places that he frequented. He uses these still now, just pointing them out to me. From having been thin as a rake and not eating, he has become almost an obsessive eater and has put on a lot of weight. He doesn't like to walk, but loves the swimming pool. Won't go in the sea, too cold, even though I swim through the summer months. He won't accompany me.

He has a sort of mentor: a friend of mine, an older man in his seventies, whom Rafi phones regularly, often several times a day. To this person Rafi will talk. He is still devoted to his brother, but frequently yells at him, a source of conflict being the Hornby train tracks, which he couldn't really manage, and which got pulled up and thrown around.

From his school for children with special needs we tried a variety of day centres. One of these was the Elham Valley Vineyard, where he would go with a carer who dropped him off and picked him up. The Vineyard is a wonderful asset, with a tea shop, a pottery, a garden centre. They also have residential facilities, and I thought I had, with this, resolved the problem of Rafi's later life. However, he put his foot down and demanded not to be taken there anymore. Fortuitously a friend of mind alerted me to a day care centre in Folkestone, which Rafi attends now and where he is very happy. They do artistic activities: there are a couple of very good artists who attend. They also create films and plays.

Rafi has got over the proto-bereavement of his brother

moving out of the house and out of this area and has also developed a sense of affection for his sister-in-law. However the attacks of retching have not altogether disappeared and occur even during the night. Oh, and did I say, with his sadness, he moved into bed with me, and didn't move out for five years? It took a fortnight away in America for me by myself, and care from his father to get him out of this.

Leo for his part, went through school with no problems, bar a slight laziness, although not in his art, which is where his real talents lie. When he left his primary school, he cried. I was touched by this. He was the only one who seemed to be so cut up on the last day. Such a tender soul. I never felt that his primary school teachers valued him, except one of them. When he got into the local grammar school on appeal, I still don't know if I was doing the right thing. I was never sure his primary school was the right choice as it never seemed to value the academic: perversely an advantage for Leo who was not academic.

He later complained of the school however that they were continually having prayers: before break, before lunch, here and there. He is quite humorous about that, as he is about the behaviour of the boys at grammar school who, he tells me, never missed a trick in criticising the Italians. He got through it though, making friends with the art teachers, who seemed to be more on his wavelength.

Leo selected psychology and history for his A levels, as well as the art he was so good at. I wonder if he chose psychology to help him deal with his brother? Both the boys were devoted to each other, and I cannot remember any arguments, bar one day when an autistic 'friend' of Rafi's came round and went up to their bedroom, and smashed up a K'Nex aeroplane that Leo had put together, with the other boy throwing the entire set of pieces around the bedroom. This was something Rafi would never have done. The boy's mother was rightly angry and ordered him to go and pick up the pieces.

In the sixth form the extent of Leo's rebellion was seen in his hair. This was a mop of blonde, well down over the collar, where it was not supposed to be. Amusingly, his father used to think, 'ah, that's my son, the rebel', until he saw Leo's companions in the band he had and all five of them had exactly the same hair-do, bar being in different colours!

From school, Leo went on to study for a Foundation course in art, where he got through without any problem, but without distinction too. He was never really a hard worker and in my opinion did not make full use of the opportunities offered him. This attitude continued into his degree course, where he was derailed in his studies by falling in love. He basically hid his light under a bushel and it is only with maturity that he works hard and is both assiduous and broad-minded, scrupulous in the work he does. For a while after university he went to clean cars, just to ensure he had a job and an income. He had been lucky. Money was set up in Trust for him, from my father's estate. He said he felt guilty about this.

Perhaps, though, I am not allowing him enough rein for his own psychological state. For three weeks when he was in Class 12, he was ill, vomiting all his meals. We took him to the GP and then on to hospital for tests and he was diagnosed with gastric problems and medicated with Zantac. The problem was nervous, however, and as the years have passed and we have talked together about his state of mind, he recalls that he had gone to the GP with anxiety, and just been told that 'it would pass,' a comment that he found singularly unhelpful. Well, the GP's other option would have been to medicate with an anti-depressive, and, as in the case of Rafi, it was considered in the end better not to do so. Eventually though he did go on a course of anti-depressants. These did not make him feel very good and he took himself off them. Now he swears by CBD as an anxiety reliever.

The most important thing in Leo's life was his decision to get married at the tender age of 23. In accordance with the mental states of the people he has been brought up with, his selected companion developed borderline personality disorder, with fibromyalgia, and despite considerable artistic talents herself, is more or less permanently indisposed.

But Rafi is better, I am stable, and Leo has a decent job. We have a precarious balance in a troubled world, a world now riven with the pandemic coronavirus. Is home the people or the place? Perhaps it is both. People in lockdown will now have time to ponder this and their enforced 'captivity'.

This book is both for my daughter-in-law and the millions of people suffering mental disorders, and for the dispossessed without home and stability. And, actually, with Covid 19, the book is for all of us.

Afterword

This book was halfway to press when a memory came back to me that seems somehow to sum up the story of my life.

I knew the philosopher Ferruccio Rossi-Landi, who was a bit of a philanderer. He invited me out on his yacht with a Hungarian couple and three young students. The students were to sail the boat, which was called *Abraxa*, after the first two letters of the names of his three daughters. It was a horrible day, grey and blustery, and as we drove to the quayside he told me that it was always a little hazardous to get back into port because the waterways were a sort of delta. He pointed out to me a ventilation tower at a factory near the bay where the boat was moored, and explained that the secret was to use the tower to orient back into the harbour.

We had left the dock and were heading out to sea when Ferruccio, who was tying or untying some rope or other, suddenly collapsed. The Hungarian, who was a poet called Jimmy, went to help him and I noticed that he was bent over Ferruccio and seemed to be praying. Ferruccio had simply dropped dead. The students immediately turned the boat around to get back to land, but the young man at the tiller was veering around all over the place. I yelled to him, 'Ferruccio said follow the tower!'

When we eventually moored without mishap and the ambulance arrived, the paramedics confirmed that Ferruccio had indeed died. The students thought he had told me about the tower with his dying breath, but in fact it was only by the merest chance that he had mentioned it as we drove down to the boat. It was just fortunate that I had paid attention. After Jimmy the poet had departed with his companion, I and the three students found it hard to leave. We held a sort of protracted wake, there on the quay, in which we stayed together remembering Ferruccio and telling stories about him.

Oddly, the man I was with at that time recounted a conversation he'd had with a Yugoslav sociologist who'd dreamed about Ferruccio's death. He practically collapsed himself when I told him the philosopher had actually died that day.

For me, if there is a lesson from this incident it's that amid the random catastrophes of life there is a value in always paying attention. Perhaps that's the secret of my survival.

Acknowledgements

This book would never have seen the light of day without support from Ros Franey, Abdulrazak Gurnah and James Essinger. Many thanks to them and also to members of my family who read early versions, Leo Crampton Dazzara and Mauro Dazzara. Thanks also to Jayne Gould who read and commented in our small writers' group (just the two of us!). To all the friends who appear in the volume: thanks for being there.

A note on the cover illustration

The cover illustration is a print by Italian/Slovene master print-maker, lithographer, teacher and mentor Franco Vecchiet, whom I was honoured to know.

It is called *In Friendship*.

I chose this abstract image because the combination of straight lines and curves, the spiky lines, reminded me of the ins and outs, the ups and downs of life. The restricted colour palette reminds me that sometimes in life it is necessary to be totally focused. The image is deceptively simple, for techniques that are sophisticated and elegant.